THE
QUARTERLY

EDITED BY

GORDON LISH

THE
QUARTERLY

2 / SUMMER 1987

VINTAGE BOOKS

A DIVISION OF RANDOM HOUSE

NEW YORK

THE QUARTERLY (ISSN 0893-3103) IS EDITED BY GORDON LISH
AND IS PUBLISHED QUARTERLY FOR $25 PER YEAR ($36.25 IN
CANADA) BY VINTAGE BOOKS, A DIVISION OF
RANDOM HOUSE, INC., 201 EAST 50TH STREET, NEW YORK,
NEW YORK 10022. APPLICATION TO MAIL AT
SECOND-CLASS POSTAGE RATES IS PENDING AT NEW YORK, N.Y.,
AND ADDITIONAL MAILING OFFICES. SEND ORDERS AND
ADDRESS CHANGES TO THE QUARTERLY, SUBSCRIPTION
DEPARTMENT, P.O. BOX 615, HOLMES, PA 19043.
THE QUARTERLY WELCOMES THE OPPORTUNITY TO READ WORK
OF EVERY CHARACTER, AND IS ESPECIALLY CONCERNED
TO KEEP ITSELF AN OPEN FORUM. MANUSCRIPTS
MUST BE ACCOMPANIED BY THE CUSTOMARY RETURN MATERIALS,
AND SHOULD BE ADDRESSED TO THE EDITOR, THE QUARTERLY,
201 EAST 50TH STREET, NEW YORK, NEW YORK 10022.
THE QUARTERLY WILL MAKE THE UTMOST EFFORT TO OFFER
ITS RESPONSE TO MANUSCRIPTS NO LATER THAN
ONE WEEK SUBSEQUENT TO RECEIPT. OPINIONS EXPRESSED
HEREIN ARE NOT NECESSARILY THOSE OF THE EDITOR
OR OF THE PUBLISHER.

ISBN: 0-394-74698-8

DESIGN BY ANDREW ROBERTS
MANAGEMENT BY DENISE STEWART AND ELLEN F. TORRON

MANUFACTURED IN THE UNITED STATES OF AMERICA

THE QUARTERLY

2 / SUMMER 1987

THE QUARTERLY

THE
QUARTERLY

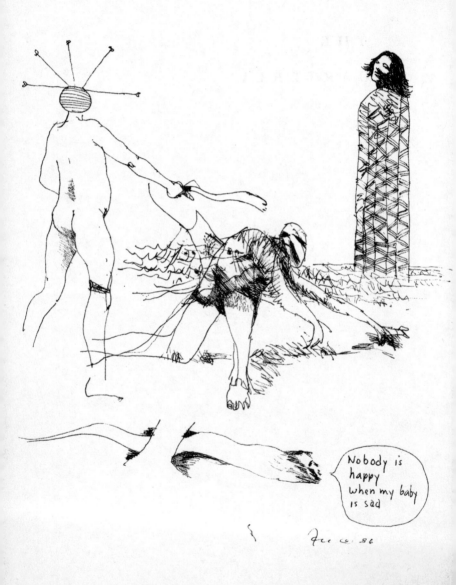

Absolution

Me and him, we're lovers. Sure, I know, he's a crazy motherfucker—and I'm the Banana Queen of Opelousas. They say I'm the prettiest since Luana Lee. But you best clap your eyes on Jimmy—he is something, too.

If you saw him down by the dirty river in his shiny turquoise truck, you'd say, *Jimmy Lucas, he's plumb got everything,* a dog in the back, banking turns, the Banana Queen right close. He'd lift a finger from the wheel, tilt his head to mean something mean. That's just the way my Jimmy is. I've seen it happen, I should know, I rode with him a lot.

Nights at the No Knees, he sets me up on the long bar. "Just look at you," he says like that, his eyes wild and proud. "You boys best come on, take a look at her. She is the Queen of Bananas."

People know about Jimmy and me. He was the first, I swear it. When I try remembering, creosote comes back best—black, black creosote, clear across my back and legs. Helps cure dry rot. I should know—I slapped it down myself, two coats heavy on the storehouse floor. Oh, I'd have been down there anyhow, watching the boys ice the trains. I tell you, it's too hot for work like that here in Opelousas. Them chunks were all of fifty pounds, nothing but hooks to hoist them with. Those boys, they were always bright with sweat.

I used to set up in the big red oak just sorting, my brain lining their half-bare bodies like down to school for supper. Jimmy was the first, I swear it. "Hey, Jimmy," I'd sing out, real softlike, just enough for me and the birds. "Hey, Jimmy."

He was pretty as a moving picture, standing splay-legged on a silver car, sweat running rivers down his back. A round, ugly fellow would come dawdling along, sticking bananas for safety's sake. "Just don't seem quite right," he'd say, eyeing the mercury like somebody's momma. "Best load her up, she's hot."

After a spell, the peel he stuck would go black like a bullet hole.

Oh, bananas.

Opelousas is the banana capital of the universe—cars and cars, clean up from Mexico City. Good seasons, those boys worked all night, throwing ice down the loud chute. Jasper always did the last of it. He was the oldest and he'd been to prison. Mind you, I never looked at Jasper. I wasn't bad as all that. I seen his bare black arms, though, veins standing out like hard-ons in church.

Momma like to drive me loopdy-looped as she is about Jimmy. "My lover Jimmy," I say front of her. "My man Jimmy."

She don't stand for it. He's a no-count. He ain't the hitching kind. He spit tobacco juice once on her kitchen floor, just like that. Oh, sweet Jesus, I know. Jimmy's got a mean streak an acre wide that puts up a fence around me, puts a little shiver in me like I just better be ready, like expect the worst, because here it's coming. But I like it.

I don't know.

I do.

When I started in on Jimmy, she like to pinch my head off. I'd get my hair done up. "How could you!" You could hear her clear in the next county. "How could you!"

Lord, my momma can carry on. Some nights, she'll be talking a blue streak upstairs, and I'll lay out, dying for the train—all those explosions right in a row, and the whistle like something to run from.

Maybe I'm a sinner to sleep naked like I do.

Sometimes I dream of fire, running stark down Jefferson with the neighbors gawking. Sometimes Momma comes in, runs her fingers up and down me. "Child of my heart," she says. "Sugar baby child, don't go."

Daddy left way back, took a liking to some Mississippi baby doll.

Folks say it's Momma I favor. But she wasn't ever Banana Queen. She ain't the contestant type. She like to laid down and get run over when Daddy brought his hussy—that's what I call her—his hussy home. I know'd it already. One day, early from school, I spied them, out at the kitchen sink, her bent down like she was spitting up, red hair spilling every which way. Strike me dead if I lie. I saw him sticking himself in her. It's the gospel truth.

I never told Momma. But she know'd, she know'd. Daddy's hussy's got a swing any fool wants for his porch. But Momma don't say nothing. She just smiles sweetlike, square in the doorway waving. Just like the Banana Queen of Opelousas.

Just like me.

Me, I aim to be remembered. That's why the Banana Queen. You can't believe how it's transporting. It hooked me Jimmy. I'd have set up in that red oak until *I* grew roots, hadn't been for this yellow crown. You should have seen appointment night, his eyes bright as fire. He come right up, clamped his hands on my face. "Ain't you something," he said. "Ain't you a precious thing."

Momma says it'll learn me vanity, being a queen and all. She says it'll make me big for my britches. I say, "Momma, tell me something I don't know already."

Momma's crazy, I can't help it.

She says when your life goes short, folks stop listening. "How many times do we get to do this?" she says.

She says, "Fetch me a glass of water."

I can't help it. I'd sleep in the woods if only I had me a big brass bed, a mess of red lipstick on a table beside. I could be queen for good, setting there like that. One day last summer Jimmy set a stuffed doll astride on a rail of fence. He took her to pieces, shot by shot, head first and feathers rising. When he got to laughing, I could see the inside of his mouth. The inside of Jimmy Lucas's mouth is a dark, vibrating place. I know.

I don't look in Momma's mouth. She's got pretty lips, but she smells like dying. I bathe her in the mornings these days. I try to help her along. I set her down in her pink tub and she wraps wet arms around my neck and whispers hard, "You should have killed me when you had a chance."

A couple years back, before I got to be queen, we was loading hay on the flatbed. This is what she means—that the Devil took hold, that I meant her to flip off the back of the truck, bales of alfalfa tumbling. She looks like that now, shiny-eyed and barely breathing, a fuse fixing to blow.

Sometimes Momma wants my mouth on her breast, like when I was her child. I lay myself down beside her, inside the darkness underneath the spread. Sometimes I think it could do me in—our nakedness, that, in my mouth, I could feel her old heart pounding. I try to help her along.

Like to make Jimmy wild, hearing this. "Don't you touch that old whore," he says. "You got to have a life of your own."

It's all of it new to me. Everybody wants something I can't figure. Jimmy wants a baby and I say, Why? The sense of it quits me. We could get us a trailer on the outskirts of town, a place where the dog could run. I just say, "No, Jimmy, no, no, no. You know I can't, Jimmy, no."

He don't stand for it. He takes me by my ankles and drags me around, my head swimming on linoleum. "Fuck you, you bitch," he says to me. "Fuck you, you cunt."

He drags me around. When he comes down on me, I think I must look like Momma, all sprawled out, head throwed back like I am coming on.

Jimmy ain't come around since Daddy come home, but he is all I can think of.

Daddy done run out of luck. We supposed he drowned in the dirty river when they found his old brown boots. But Daddy ain't been drowning, only getting fat.

"Where you been, Daddy?" I say through the screen.

He looks like some old boy I never knew in school.

"Oh, here and yonder. Best let me in."

But I don't hardly budge.

"What you been doing, Daddy?"

He gives a little shrug like *plenty*.

"Watching the grasshoppers spit," he says, and then just stands there, fatter than fat, sucking at the gaps in his teeth.

Momma sets bolt up in back of me, spewing linchpinned to the flagpole and millions of dollars. She is Queen of Nonsense now, and that gives her the right.

"She ain't saying nothing, Daddy. Don't mean a thing. What can I do for you?"

He says, "I just come to set for a spell."

I say, "Uh-huh. Ain't no reason to live in hell and have to wind up there, too. Why don't you just get along?"

He's nothing but a shadow against the screen, and from where I stand, flies disappear in him. I say, "You had your chance, old man. Momma's got a thing with God now."

It's all I can do to keep my hands from myself. Jimmy come by, just shuffled up kind of hanging his head, making a ghost on the screen. I've seen it happen, I know'd it was coming.

"Jimmy," I say, "how them bananas?"

He says, "I had me a dream. I was looking for you. I was down yonder on the blacktop ridge, hollering every way from Sunday. You wasn't hearing a thing. You was down in the long valley in a little old house with a white light. You was all prettied up and your lips were red and you was just setting, looking at me, not seeing a thing, not listening."

Ought to be something for a girl to say, but my mouth refuses me.

"Come on, child," he says. "I can't dawdle around. I got me a life to live."

"Uh-huh," I say. "Tell me about it, lover boy."

"Tell me what it's like," Momma says. "Tell me what it feels like to feel like a queen."

"Momma," I say, "Kiwanis makes six hundred twenty-eight pounds of banana pudding every year, and every year those boys come up from down the road apiece and go to pissing in the yellow vat. It feels a little like that, I guess—like everyone's happy to have you, but you got some secret stinking inside."

Any time she finds sleep, Momma goes to smiling and kissing the air. I got a notion she looks like me, practicing love in the glass. *Am I doing this right? Do I look okay?*

I been making ready since way back when, but—Momma, she can still turn me inside out. When she came up last night from that crazy spell, she took my face like she ain't laid eyes maybe for years on me.

She said, "Oh, my beloved child. I thought I was living forever in that green, tumbling place."

It was like I'd never seen her before, like she was the light of another world.

"Here," she said, "put your hand here."

She splayed my fingers across her belly. She said, "I'm all of me gone from there," and pressed my hand to prove it.

"Listen," she said. "Don't matter nohow. It's God done the things that ever get done. God made them boys piss in the pudding, ain't nothing to do with you."

Father, forgive.

If I ever flew, it would feel like this, like the earth was just something long gone. I got a big heart and can hold my breath, and when I go deep in this black, black river, my whole body disappears. I can feel water wanting me. I know it's a sin, but

I open my legs. I shout Jimmy's name so it turns to music by the time that it finds air.

Oh, ain't it a shame, my sweet, sweet Jimmy. I could have loved you good.

Father, forgive.

I lay out nights dying for the train. I lay on my back, and the thing goes growing inside me, up in my gut, around and around my secret parts. It has a life of its own, and surely the hunger of a hundred horses. It is a thing of the flesh, child of the Devil, who split my Momma's pretty lips and spilt himself in her. Surely now is the time for prayer. Dear God, sweet God, pray God. What's my momma ever done to you? You listen to me. Ain't no kind of life you're lending her.

I got the skirling sound of a train smack between my ears. It goes, *Take me. Take me,* it goes. *Take me, take me, take me, take me.*

Do I have to do all your filthy work?

Have you spent up all your Amazing Grace?

You think I know better, but you got me wrong—I ain't afraid of you. You can have this no-count soul to keep. Suit yourself. Do what you will. Tickle me pink. I can't use it. Glory be, and to the Father, and to the Holy Son. I'd let Momma sprawl on the shimmying track.

You got your doubts.

I'd say, *Go on, go on. Get on with it, Momma. Let's be done with this thing.* **Q**

On the Rope

I have to tell my uncle it is just a bread wrapper, a crubbly piece of paper thrown up on the fence by the wind. I run out to show that is all it is, but the spell is already on my uncle. When I come back in from showing, it is just as well I should have stayed outside.

My gramere says the barge they brought down the bayou coming to get my uncle and his boat slid up on the edge of our backyard. She said the barge slid up in the darkness with the floodwaters boiling under its bow and she said God was giving her a warning, saying, See how that barge is boiling like it is a man's head showing out of a pot the man is boiling in. She said she could hear the water boiling like the water was hot and she said the way the water boiled around the bow it looked like the barge was coming closer, but that it was her will keeping it away, pushing it from coming into our backyard and taking away my uncle and his boat.

Some men in green uniforms used a crane to hoist my uncle's boat up onto the barge. My uncle was afraid they would scratch the finish. When my uncle came back from where the floodwaters had boiled away everything from the land, he did not care what the boat looked like. Gramere said the boat looked like it had been whipped with wires, like it had gone on the barge and been whipped with wires, and my uncle looked like the men in the green uniforms had made him do it. She said my uncle could not look at the boat, like when a man is drunk and whips a dog for no good reason and then when he is sober he cannot look at it, even though he is a man and it is a dog. That is how my uncle could not look at his boat.

My uncle said at first when the barge stopped and the men in the green uniforms let his boat into the water he thought they had gone too far south, like the floodwaters had flooded them all the way out into the Gulf. He said in the night all you could see was the amber light on the bow of the barge and all you could hear was the sound of the floodwaters boiling all around, boiling away everything from the face of the earth.

My uncle said all that night he drove his boat over the boiling waters wondering why the men in the green uniforms had put him so far out into the Gulf, until in the shine of his flashlight he saw an island of sparkling diamonds. When my uncle drove his boat over to the island he saw it was the crown of a tree boiling in the currents of the floodwaters and the diamonds were the eyes of all the snakes spun up through the branches. My uncle said the snakes dropped into water so they could swim over and crawl into his boat, but instead they were swept away into the darkness by the boiling waters. My uncle said after that he was careful of the islands and was not fooled by their diamond shining lights.

My uncle said that when the sun was supposed to come up it did not come up at all but just it started to rain harder. The rain got into my uncle's breath when he drove his boat. He had to hold his hand over his mouth like he was going to call a duck, but he was breathing in through the tube he made with his fingers instead of blowing out with his tongue. That was when the Brahma bull went by backward. The way it went by with just its head out of the water holding up its long, flat horns, my uncle said it looked like a big brown bird made of solid wood gliding over the boiling water looking for its breakfast. My uncle drove his boat alongside the Brahma bull and he looped some ski rope around the long, flat horns, but he said it did not work too well trying to pull the Brahma bull back to the barge because sometimes the ski rope pulled down on the Brahma bull's head so its long, thin horns dipped into the water, and sometimes the Brahma bull's nose blew out water instead of breath, and by the time my uncle got over to where the barge seemed to be moving toward him, the ski rope was going straight down into the water by my uncle's boat, like it held an anchor my uncle could not pull up. When the men in the green uniforms asked my uncle what it was, he said it was nothing, and he cut the ski rope loose from his boat and set out over the boiling waters again.

When it was supposed to be noon my uncle said he found the baby on the rope. He said it looked like somebody had tied a strong rope around the baby's waist and was still holding on, because the other end seemed deep down in the water. The baby was cutting through the current with its arms and head thrown back like it had just broken up to the surface to take a long deep breath that it was still taking. My uncle said when he pulled on the rope from where it went deep into the water, it did not feel like it gave as much as it felt like it was being let go of. When my uncle got back to the barge with the baby on the rope, the men in the green uniforms gave him some coffee and a doughnut and a Spam sandwich. He said the doughnut dissolved and the Spam sandwich washed away and the coffee tasted like rain.

My uncle said the girl swimming on the barbed-wire fence had skin that did not come off in his hands like the skin on some of the others did. He said when he first saw her, her right arm was crooked over her head and her left arm was following, with her head turned like she was a brave swimmer in the boiling waters, making it look like she was stroking away from where everything was being boiled off the face of the earth. He said he was shouting at her to swim, to come on and swim, as he drove his boat over to her. He said even as he unstuck her from the barbed-wire fence he talked to her and looked away from her modesty, because her clothes had been boiled away, so he just focused on a little mark on her cheek like a snakebite the barbed wire had made that did not bleed because all her blood had boiled away, too. He made himself over her, protecting her modesty until they got back to the barge and the men in the green uniforms helped hand her up from my uncle's boat so they could lay her on top of the other boiled-over people they had stacked at one end of the barge like corded wood.

My uncle said that after three days, when the only sun was

just the amber light, the barge was full. The men in the green uniforms headed it back up the bayou, and even though sometimes they would see things hung up in the trees and on the fences they would not stop. The men in the green uniforms spread white powder out of green barrels on the people stacked like corded wood under the big green tarps. Men's boats like my uncle's were laid helter-skelter on the barge, roughed up like a lot of toys some bullies had come along and played too rough with. All the men like my uncle who had the boats stood around the edges of the barge away from the big green tarps, away from their boats they could not look at, and as far away from one another as they could without falling over into the boiling water. They stood watching for faces of boiled-over people to come up to just below the surface like they sometimes did, like they just wanted to sneak a peek before slipping away back under. They stood looking away to the trees and to the fences along the bayou that caught the boiled-over people. They stood looking, giving good hard long looks, because they knew, like my uncle knew, that once they were back up the bayou they would never be able to watch a stew pot boil, or look at something caught on barbed wire ever the same again, even with someone like me coming in to show it is nothing but a crubbly piece of nothing thrown up on the fence by the wind. **Q**

I Want to Know the Answer

I had with me this woman. I said, Are you prepared to accept sexual fidelity to me until we can be together in paradise? She didn't answer right away. She wanted to think about it. I didn't mind that. I'd taken a long time to arrange this question in my mind before I asked it of her. Things took time. I knew that. I'd taken the time and still the question had not come out the way I'd arranged it. One thing I knew was that I had to have her answer before I left her on this street corner, before I left this town this evening. I had to leave town this evening, there was no taking time about that.

Will you be sexually faithful to me until we can be together in paradise? That's what I had meant to ask. How I meant to say it. So I said it again, I grabbed her arm and I said it. Will you? She was walking a little faster now and I had to take a stride or two to get myself abreast of her and I had to grab her arm. Will you? Her head whipped over at me, her head whipped back, she tried to free that arm. She looked like a shaggy dog to me in that second, in that instant when her eyes were confronting mine. Like a shag rug, a piece cut out, piece from the floor you and maybe a hundred others, say a family of four, had walked on, trod on, for forty or fifty years, never a cleaning; then a little piece cut out and maybe flapped a few times to shake out the sticks, the big stuff, and then fitted up over her naked head so she'd look human. A brown carpet, filthy, I said that. Anyway, that's how she looked, not nice, not nice, not the least bit nice, not in that second. She was nice, but not in that second. She didn't look like anyone who would ever be sexually faithful. I saw that in the second her head turned. When I was a boy—but wait, I'm not falling into that trap, not in that "when I was" trap. That trap—you're walking along, I'm walking along, and I can see that "when I was" trap in front of me before my foot steps down, the same way Tarzan could see a pool of quicksand. Quicksand. Tarzan could always see, he was always aware of, where the quicksand was. If it was anywhere in his jungle, in his jungle, he knew it. Snakes were different. Snakes were the one thing different in the jungle. In the jungle they'd drop down on you from a tree, on Tarzan, I mean, from a tree. And *you* saw it coming, you always did, but Tarzan never. Tarzan never. He had a blind side, but you yourself, you didn't have this particular blind side. No, you didn't. You were A-O.K. on the snakes and the blind-side question. My mom now, Mom now, she was all blind side. In a jungle she wouldn't have lasted a minute. The snakes would have eaten her alive. You know what I mean. Quicksand, okay, snakes not okay, they'd squeeze her to death in a minute. So I asked her, this one, I asked her—I was within my right and I asked her—How do you feel about sexual congress? We've done that, we've had that—but how do you feel about sexual fidelity? Now, that's one that will get you, it will drop down on you from a tree and squeeze out your breath in a minute. I knew this. I was born knowing this. I only had to look at my mother. You come to life chained to your mother's bed. You do, but that is not what I am saying. Okay, reconsider, maybe it is. You're chained to that bed, but you're chained there by the snake, that's what I mean, and I don't mean the snake you may think I mean, I mean the snake that always went after Tarzan. That's how they do it. And they don't use that snake from the Tarzan movie either, because you can see that snake coming before Tarzan can. It's a particular kind of snake, this one, you can't see it. But it's got you shackled. You can feel it squeezing your bones.

Once, I was in bed, I was about nine years old, in this bed, my mother's bed, I was down at the foot of the bed, across the bed, and my father and mother were in the bed, too. They were in the bed the other way, the right way, and I was at the foot of the bed and I heard her say, Don't wake him. You better not wake him. I ought not to let you do this, don't do this. Don't do it. She was whispering but I heard her, although at that time, at that time, I didn't know it was my father she was saying this to because at this time I didn't know it was my father in this bed. All I knew is that I was at the foot of the bed, the wrong way in the bed, and that two other people were in the bed. My head was under the covers, a cold night, a freezing night, and I could smell their feet. Feet, that's all, that's all I smelled.

I shouldn't let you do this, that's what she said. I didn't hear him say anything. I never heard him say anything. The whole time he didn't say anything and I was listening, I want to tell you I was listening, I was still as a bullet and listening. But my father never said anything, not one word. He rolled up over her, you see, and the mattress shook, the mattress shivered, and she said, You better not wake him. It was too late, wasn't I listening? Wasn't I smelling their feet? Wasn't I? I was. He didn't say anything. Not one word. He never had. I thought to myself, Why is he here? Where did he come in from? Who is he, anyway? And the mattress went on shaking. It went on forever shaking. His feet kept poking me. Both his feet kept poking me. The cold bottoms of his feet, poke, poke. He had his feet against me because I was his brace. He was using me as his brace as he did this with my mother, and what was happening was I was being shoved right down between the foot of the mattress and the heel of the bed frame. There was a space there, a hole, and he was shoving his feet against me and that's where I was going, into that hole. She kept saying, "Shhh," that's what she kept saying. "Shhh, don't wake him, I'm a fool to let you be doing this," that's what she kept saying.

"You'll be gone in the morning, you better be gone in the morning," yes, she said that.

It went on forever. It did, it was forever, don't tell me it wasn't. You'd see those people in the Tarzan stepping off into the quicksand, running into the quicksand, you'd see their shoulders, then only the head, their eyes, and what would you see next? A hat up there on top of the bubbling sand. Then not even the hat. That's what you would see. That's what I would see, and you too, if we went to the same movie. All my friends, we saw the same movie, we'd come out into the sunlight and we'd say, "Did you see that hat? Did you see that hat? Boy, I'm staying away from quicksand," that's what we'd say. "Quicksand's not going to get me."

"Shhh, don't wake him."

What I'm saying is, Where'd he come from? He hadn't been around in years and years. He never said anything. Never. He just put his feet against me and pushed. There were these covers, these heavy covers, I told you that. The feet. You had to have all these covers, the freezing cold, so my head is under there.

I don't know what I was doing in her bed in the first place. I had my own bed, but I guess what happened is—wait now, this is how it was. I had my bed and then he'd come home, he'd come back, out of the blue, my father had, he'd just knocked on the door and come on in, come on up those stairs and sat down and somehow he'd got my bed. That's right, he had to have my bed because she wasn't having him in her bed, that's one possible way it happened, but why it was I was down at the foot of the bed, across the bed, you'll just have to make up your own explanation for that. His feet were all over me. That's what I hated worse, his feet, all that pushing.

"I shouldn't let you," I hated that, too.

Grit your teeth. That's what you do. That's what I was doing, gritting my teeth, the same as I was doing when I said to her this sexual fidelity question. Paradise matters. You want to get there, you have to ask it. Will you be sexually faithful to me until we can reach paradise? I've told you, she wanted to think about this. She didn't want to answer right away. And I wasn't rushing her. Let her grit her teeth while she thinks about it. Let her think she can run. It isn't the right question, that's what she was saying to herself. I bet you a dollar that was it. I better watch this guy, that's what she was saying. There we were, out in the night, we've settled on the price, we've established that, we've done it to everyone's satisfaction, done it *as agreed,* and here comes along this question out of the blue. Fifty dollars, you think I ever meant her to keep that fifty dollars? You're crazy. I don't deal in that kind of craziness. She keeps it, she answers the question. It's that simple. I can see quicksand coming, see that hat, and I don't deal in either. I don't deal in hats. Hats are fuck-all, that's how I feel about hats. Paradise, that's another question. Paradise, now that I think of it, is the *only* question. There is no other question. In the whole of the universe. You can be down under the covers, under a thousand blankets, under quicksand, and that's the question. Where's paradise? Where's sexual fidelity, too? Okay, that's another one. Maybe there are more questions, after all. I don't care how many questions there are. Questions, any you can think of, can go the way of that hat. They can go right down. They can go down where you never see them because they came to you so long ago, and were answered so long ago, that now it's as if you've come out of the movie and you're standing around with your friends, asking these things, but what you're really saying is, What can we do now? We've seen the movie, what can we do now? Go back home? Are you kidding? You're wanting me to go back home? You're crazy.

Okay, so after some years what you find yourself thinking about as you leave the movie is sexual favors. She doesn't look cheap. No, they've never looked cheap, not to me. What they look like is that they are going to cost you your life. They are going to cost you the whole of it. One way or another. I don't care about the fifty dollars, what's fifty dollars, fifty dollars is nothing in the grand scheme of the universe, it's zilch and nothing when it comes to the final payoff. We've agreed on the final payoff, and fifty dollars is nothing, not even if you've got to have it up front. "Up front, baby, or I don't move," that's what this one said. "I don't move from this corner." We've both been around, we've got no argument. To hell with fifty dollars, I say, I say that, but what I say too, pretty soon, after we've done it, after we've done it *in the manner agreed* and in accordance with the purchase price, is, What next? What do we do next? What do I do? You can't go home. You can't get into paradise. Not right away, so what do you do?

You ask for something. It seems to me it isn't asking too much to expect a little sexual fidelity before or until you get there. That's what I mean. That's what I'm saying. So you put the question to her. *I—me—I—I* put the question to her because I know you wouldn't. You can never be counted on to put the question to her, whereas I don't mind doing it. I do it for you, I'm accustomed. "Can I expect you to be faithful to me until we reach paradise?" There is only one question and that's it, that's the one, and it's what we are all wanting to know.

Okay, she grits her teeth.

She yanks that arm.

She's thinking it over. She didn't see it coming, there's this weirdo beside her, maybe he's got this knife at her throat and maybe he hasn't, but the answer better be the right one, that's what I'm saying. It better be, because I'm not here to hurt. I'm not here to inflict pain or cause trouble. It's just that I want to know. I want to know the answer.

Tell me. **Q**

Dune Trek

[1]

A sentry is walking up and down singing a song in Spanish. He is a private in the Spanish Foreign Legion. He has got red tassels at both peaks of his cap. He has got red piping on his uniform. On his left arm under his sleeve he has a snake tattoo, it also has daggers. He's singing to keep himself awake. A song about a woman in Villafranca and how he walked up and down beneath her balcony in the rain. A strong sense of *forsakenness* often overcomes people in the Sahara.

Inside the sentry hut, the relief watch is making a fire on a shovel. Three cups, he says: one for life, one for love, and one for the next caravan out of Al Aiuún, which leaves only on Thursdays.

Al Aiuún means *the eye.* A spring is the eye of the desert. Interesting facts: "Every day the desert grows by forty square miles, and two hundred people die as a direct or indirect consequence."

Everybody waits all night in the sentry hut. At dawn the trucks will pull up; they're coming from Villa Cisneros loaded with tea, with cone sugar, with camel saddles, bales of blue cloth, figs with strange, white, threadlike worms in them, and goat cheese in salty hide containers. At 6 A.M. it will be very cold and the drivers will be smoking black tobacco, their sleeves pulled down over the five watches they wear on each arm. They are smuggling the watches into Morocco, and under each front seat there will be a lot of cassette recorders, same deal. They like smuggling things into Morocco. It's fun. The drivers appear to have glittering Rolex angel arms, they will be calling to each other: Did you see that whore last night in the cabaret?

[2]

At the edge of the oasis is a quonset hut; it is a cabaret for the Legion and the army officers. A thin, tired, clumsy Hassanayeen woman was dancing. On her layers of flimsy yellow-and-pink robes was a printed design which seemed to be composed of fish and roses. "Mustafa" is a strange melody, somehow it is both fake and authentic, it is actually haunting. It's like necromancy—dead people are liable to show up to listen, smacking their lips. One thing about officers is that they always get paid. Earlier in the afternoon three of them in a jeep with machine guns picked up the photographer and went off somewhere with him. I waited for the sound of distant shots. How was I going to get out of the Sahara by myself? On reflection it appeared to be either impossible or dangerous. But they brought him back. They were just checking his papers. Sound of distant shots: rifle practice. They brought him back on Wednesday, and in the bar of the cabaret there were a lot of videogames with X-ray-blue lights that emitted the sounds of gunfire and accelerating machines. People like to check your papers. They like the *white sound* of papers and the photographs.

The sentry is walking up and down singing about Villa-franca and the rain, about being under the bizarre black trees that make wet designs like fish bones in the rain. A man in a downpour, full of love or desire or simply a kind of emotional greed, this is what his song is about. *Mi amor.* About experience. Demonology, non-electronic.

Al Aiuún means *the eye.* Interesting facts: "Many persons who have had the experience of traveling across a desert report constant feelings of anxiety and forlornness during the journey. A feeling of having been *forsaken* overtakes one." There is only one bar in Al Aiuún, the officers' cabaret, and somebody plays "Mustafa" on a trumpet, and a tired, possibly hungry Hassanayeen woman takes off her clothes, revealing her body, which is a dark design of fish and roses. The Foreign Legionnaires have snake tattoos and pasts and debts. Some of them don't even watch her take off her clothes. Go sit in the sentry hut to wait for the caravan to form up and listen to the sentry sing about Villafranca in the rain, *mi amor, yo te quiero,* and so on, the rain, *la lluvia.*

Leaning against the wall of the sentry hut, I look at the relief watch making a pot of tea on the fire in the shovel, staring at the other life forms sitting around on the dirt floor. Against the other wall five Hassanayeen men in blue robes and black turbans are also observing; they seem like suspicious blue hallucinations or raptors. Their eyes move in fragmented sections, as if following the invisible movements of remote vehicles which only they can hear.

They have turned off the Arabic music coming through their transistor radios in order to listen to the sentry singing, in his frail Spanish voice, that if she doesn't lean out of the balcony only once and acknowledge him, standing under all that dangerous antique ironwork, in the rain, he'll go and join the Foreign Legion. He's lucky Spain still has a foreign legion. After they are thrown out of the Sahara they will have left only Al Hoceima, Ceuta, and Melilla. The sentry thinks, "I don't want to be transferred to Al Hoceima, there are centipedes up there as long as your socks, and at night they slowly march up your blankets, smacking their lips."

Outside, by herself, sits the woman who was dancing at the cabaret for the officers. Nobody talks to her. The men ask the photographer, What was my bride-price? He tells them a thousand English pounds. The relief watch makes tea on a shovel and I feel as if I am worth a thousand pounds English. Throw in a few goats. Take off one shoe and pour out the sand, take off the other shoe and pour out the sand, don't look anybody in the eye. *Mi amor, yo te quiero.*

[3]

Interesting facts: "The desert is expanding exponentially. The people who are the most affected are those who live on the fringes of the Sahara. Sandstorms occur with increasing frequency. The frightful famines that have visited Africa in recent years are only a ghastly prelude to a series of famines that will descend on humanity in the next several decades. Africa is a drying continent, over which the desert is continuing its inexorable advance."

Thursday continues its inexorable advance. The caravans are allowed to leave only on those mornings, to travel through an area mapped out in grids by the Spanish Army; hungry people are dangerous. A safe-conduct pass is issued to all foreign travelers; it has your photograph on it, taken with a flash, making you look as if you had been hit by lightning. Ancient fish bones make patterns in the rocks like Berber tattoos. Clouds are running up out of the Atlantic in long, dry lines, pure Sahara electronic clickings, digital clouds running right to left like Kufic script. The sentries handle their rifles carelessly, as if they were umbrellas. The brass rings that hold the webbing straps to the stocks glitter nervously in the firelight.

There are three cups, the sentry says: one for life, which is sweet; one for love, which is sweeter; and one for death, for after death is paradise and that is sweetest of all. Necromancy. Sand slithers in under the door like a sudden thought, creepy and pale.

At least, that's what the sentry claims the Arabs say, over their tea; he states this confidently and actually smiles as he hands the glasses around. The men in blue robes don't like to be told what Arabs say, especially by infidels; these are desert Arabs and what they know of European thought is the presence of soldiers, canned milk, alcohol, digital watches, Italian Western movies, and other filth. One of the men gets up, opens the door, and spits violently into the sand. Clouds are running up out of the west like shuttlecocks, white and dry. The dunes, too, are smooth, they lie without moving as shadows run across them in fugitive, demented dreams.

I get up and go outside. The sentries have loaded rifles and I have an odd feeling, as if I weighed a thousand pounds.

[4]

One of the men gets up, opens the door, and spits violently into the sand. "The desert is called *bahr bela ma,* sea without water." At five miles the curvature of the earth becomes apparent and things, short things, disappear below the horizon. There are the smaller dunes, called barkhans, which are migrating dunes shaped like a sickle. They often travel across the desert in lines more than sixty miles long. The drivers never know where to expect them; every Thursday they have changed, because the dunes migrate on Wednesdays as well. The drivers run around the edges of the barkhans, trying to stay on the hammada, a gravelly, stony floor of fragmenting pebbles. "Then there are the great star dunes, which can reach a thousand feet and do not move; they can serve for many years as landmarks." It has been five years since it rained. The desert is expanding exponentially.

At five miles the curvature of the earth intervenes, and when we leave at dawn we and all the other short things will disappear below the sentries' horizon. Arabic music in the background gives an intense, sinister feeling to these occurrences. It is just before dawn. Everything the moon says is true. Ramadan migrates through the calendar, the month of hunger. Outside the military perimeter, the beautiful dunes have no color and migrate in long lines like free traders bringing famine. Don't like that, do you? says the sentry to the man who went outside to spit. That's what you people say, isn't it? Death is sweetest of all?

All this is going on in Spanish and I get up and go outside. The photographer doesn't understand Spanish, but I don't warn him. I hardly know him. He's come up all the way from Mauritania; he keeps his eyes on the steam from the glass of tea. I can't tell you how cold it is. Stars stare straight down through the atmosphere, curious and alien. In the cabaret the soldiers are putting fifty-peseta coins in the videogames; one of these games appears to be a caravan of eight trucks running across the hammada, which you, the pilot, try to catch in a crossfire.

[5]

The woman who took her clothes off and has Berber fish-bone tattoos on her chin is leaning against the outside wall of the sentry hut, because the men won't let her come in. She's a whore. She's playing with a digital watch with the sweet, pleased fascination of a small child. She has looked in the window of the hut and has seen the brass armbands the men are wearing. Maybe that's why she's outside. Inside the windings of the brass wire little pieces of paper are tucked in; there are certain verses from the Koran written on these papers and these special verses have the magical property of protecting the wearer from bullets. Sorcery, very freaky. This means after they take the caravan into the desert on Thursday they assume they are going to be shot at, at least by Friday. By whom is an interesting question. Don't ask, don't look at the wrong people, we will be in Morocco by a week from Sunday. The woman is very dirty and very thin. One of the men comes outside and spits violently into the sand.

Then I come out. This is the way it works: Only saints and bandits know how unimportant is the human body. Include soldiers. The pair is the smallest unit in which the more highly developed life forms can endure cosmic dimensions, and what you have here—the Sahara, the famine, the war—is cosmic dimensions. I sit down beside the woman and hand her a tin of sardines. She jams it instantly into her robes.

Riding on top of the load of sugar and tea and bales of blue cloth tomorrow I will look up into the sky, and you know what?

We are hanging upside down on the bottom of the planet, staring with intrepid unconcern into outer space. I will be overcome by a feeling both passive and suicidal, you want to jump. The dancer/whore will have pulled her seven veils over her head against the tearing wind. A sudden, soundless avalanche of sand occurs on a distant cliff face; the whole face falls off. Cosmic. As a child, I used to try to love God but at the same time I was afraid He would lean down out of heaven and take a bite out of my head. Al*lah*, says the man who came outside. He goes back in and sits down. Famine has become normal and the other thing is that I hardly know the photographer and I wonder if he's planning on going off on his own when we reach Tantan. The sentry's song makes it sound as if he were soaked and dripping, drowning in a downpour in a little Iberian square in Villafranca. The woman who took off her clothes in the cabaret plays with a kind of beeper on her digital watch, listening to it intently. The sun is about to come up. Everything the sun says is true, and it is referred to as "she" in Arabic. We are at the perimeter, and back in the white, rounded domes of the oasis town, you can see the old fort, radio aerials rising like fish bones.

[6]

There are places in the Sahara where only microorganisms can exist. I find this interesting but strange, and actually frightful. Ahead of us is four hundred miles to the nearest water. The photographer says in Tantan they sell it by the cup, one for day and one for night and one for the curvature of the earth, where at five miles you disappear below the horizon with all the other short things that are either short naturally or short because they are collapsing and can no longer stand. At the next plateau we pass tomorrow, an entire cliff face will disappear. All across the peach-colored dunes *miradores* like lighthouses stand up; they are watching the expanding and dangerous desert with rectangular green eyes, which are radar, and the little radar screens make faint crackling noises as we move across them, green dots on time and on Thursday, with all our passes in order. Arabic music forms an intense, sinister background, the volume turned up. In the middle of the desert people draw together, a sense of having been *forsaken* manifests itself. The sky has become lower at dawn; little spongy gray clouds tear past at eight thousand feet, running right to left like Arabic script. At this point I am absolutely unacquainted with anybody else's body, not the outside body, but the inside body, which is a great star dune, the color of a peach, solid and immutable. It's just a matter of staying close to the photographer, his body is a windbreak. Yesterday he got taken away by several men with machine guns in a jeep and I ran after him down the narrow, blazing streets; the fear of being *forsaken* overtakes people in the hammada. In a small room in Tantan, in the inn, the fonduk, I will look up and see the photographer watching me in the mirror. All the other short things will have disappeared below the curvature of the pure Sahara with its electronic clickings, a vast videogame we are programmed to lose, and the woman dancer with the fish-bone Berber tattooing on her chin is a kind of demented singular unit; she and her robes printed with fish and roses will disappear into the streets of Tantan, keeping on toward Morocco, where people are not so hungry. Famine is a state of absence, but the desert is growing exponentially, filling up the hungry places and the sickle-shaped barkhans the way free traders offer their soft yellow wares from oasis to oasis, from Villa Cisneros, to Al Aiuún, to Tantan and Sidi Ifni, and are reaching up to Béni Mellal.

As a city, Tantan is almost totally yellow.

[7]

Interesting facts: "One incident will serve to demonstrate how powerful the grinding action of sand can be. After forty-eight hours of a hurricane-force sandstorm, the glass in all the vehicles had become opaque from the sandblasting and the windshields had to be knocked out before the journey could continue."

In the middle of the journey everything we are carrying will assume enormous importance, the cameras, the dried figs, the tin of sardines, the goat cheese. The water bags, made of goatskin, shaped like goats. I will look back and see our tracks running backward toward Al Aiuún, proof that we have a past, and a future, where I will make more tracks. The tracks go back through time to the Islands, Europe, North America, and assure me I must have had a beginning.

We will pass a man whose three camels are lying in the stony gravel of the hammada, perhaps dead. We will pass him at sixty miles an hour. The melody of "Mustafa" forms a manic background to the caravan's race from Al Aiuún to water, and every minute we are seduced in the arms of the barkhans, their silken, slippery sands, and throw down the sand tracks and dig out again and again, is several more pints of water lost. The body is a water clock. Planes will pass by overhead, very low, violent archangels with snake tattoos. Enfamined people are listening to pointless songs on electronic devices, and people who are hungry are often dangerous, or dying. The actual physical body of the photographer assumes enormous importance and assures me I must have a presence. He leans against the whitewashed wall of the room in the fonduk, and when I look up from the water basin, I will see him watching me in the mirror. Listen to what I'm telling you. Sidi Ifni is now almost completely deserted.

The trucks are gunning their motors, a bright avalanche prepared to accelerate into the Sahara. We climb up the slats of the sides; they are big red Mercedes, hot as forges. The dawn wind tears sideways through our loose clothing. Throw in everything, jump in after, the soldiers are coming around and I hold out my safe-conduct, which rattles and tears. The death rate is growing by almost two hundred people a day and short things keep disappearing below the curvature of the earth. We shoot forward into the Sahara, I have fallen back upon hard times and cone sugar, the Berber dancer bursts out laughing, spongy gray clouds run up on this Thursday out of the Atlantic, and for ten shocking minutes, rain falls. **Q**

SANFORD CHERNOFF

My Man at the Station

My train is late, later than usual getting in this evening.
I was dozing. My mouth is dry and half my newspaper is on the
floor. I gather it up, shuffle out to the platform (an open,
ground-level affair out here), and am heading for my car when
he approaches me.

He's a graying, not unattractive man in seersucker, which,
I notice, is badly creased at one lapel. He has obviously mis-
taken me for someone else. I was going to say something to
this effect, but he's already using my first name and talking
about my lawn. It has been giving me trouble lately, though it
seems incredible to me that he should know this.

Except for the nursery I give my business to, and my
closest neighbors, I can't think of a soul I have so much as
mentioned the lawn to.

"You're not doing yourself any good, Dave," he's saying,
referring to the fertilizer I've been using, with what I detect
now to be a lisp. "You can see that."

In my entire life, I don't believe I've come across a single
person you could actually say had a lisp. There have been a few
stammerers, and this one guy in accounting I lunch with every
once in a while salivates over certain vowels.

"A complete waste of time, you can see that."

I nod.

"Takes all the life out of it."

We're at my car. He's not through. He's suggesting
another fertilizer, one with less nitrogen content. He wants
to jot it down for me. I tell him it isn't necessary, I'll remember.

"You're sure?"

I don't care for his smile here, a bit too chummy, if you
know what I mean. I thank him cheerlessly, offer him a lift.

"I have my car." He indicates a vintage Hudson, parked

opposite the station, and asks again if I am sure about the fertilizer.

"Absolutely."

There are, of course, those people you run into now and then, and never can place. But he is not one of them. You'd remember him. Which is not to say my memory is anything to speak of. I have trouble with my social-security number and, if not for Edna (my wife), anniversaries would go unnoticed. Edna has a head for that sort of thing. I've heard her rattle off entire sections of the village charter (she's considered something of a voice in the politics around here), and it wouldn't surprise me, now that I come to think of it, if my man at the station wasn't connected with one of her committees or something.

She's on the phone when I come in and I don't get a chance to talk to her until dinner. Dinner, whenever I am this late, is a dismal business. The others (I have a girl and two boys) have already had theirs, and it is just Edna and me.

She's eaten but will take coffee with me. A nice gesture, considerate and all that, but I still wish she wouldn't. I wish she wouldn't just sit there, not quite centered in her chair, looking as if she was serving some sort of penance. It isn't necessary. She doesn't have to sit there, not for me, I've often wanted to tell her. But I don't know how. I don't see how I can without hurting her. There is very little I can tell her, it occurs to me, without hurting her. Oddly, the idea has no effect on me one way or the other, and I dig right into my pork chop. Edna turns to the centerpiece, fingers it, says that from my description the man at the station could have been anyone.

I disagree, remind her of the lisp, the Hudson. But I can see she's not interested. She sees that I see, apologizes, and, after a sip from her cup, says it's Jules.

Jules is our younger boy. He has taken it into his head lately not to come out of his room. He's been up there a full week now, leaving only for the bathroom and, Edna suddenly recalls, once to get something up from the cellar.

"What do you suppose it was?"

I have no answer.

"You're not worried?"

I don't like the idea of his missing school, but I can't say I'm worried.

"What can you say?" Her voice is quick but controlled, maybe even a bit softer.

"You could stop bringing him his food."

She's fooling with the centerpiece again, asks if I am aware of the suicide rate in children Jules's age.

"Are you serious?"

"I'm worried."

"I'll talk to him."

"You've talked to him."

"I'll talk to him again."

On the weekend I work on the lawn. I get the fertilizer and do everything just as the man at the station said. It is not that warm a day, but before I'm through I am well into a sweat. I shower and prepare to go over some reports I brought home from the office. It's been a hectic quarter. I make myself a drink and am going to sit down when I hear something fall upstairs. There is no one in the house, with the exception of Jules, of course, so I go straight up to him.

He is slow answering the door, doesn't open it. I want to know if he's all right. He says he is, and that's all he'll say.

"What was it?" I ask him.

"What was what?"

He's playing with me and I'll be damned if I am going to let him. "Jules!"

"Yes," he sings.

"Let me in."

"What for?"

"Do I need a reason?"

He doesn't answer me.

"Julie."

Still nothing from him.

"You've got your mother half crazy with all this, you know."

He says he knows.

     I keep looking for my man with the lisp. In a restaurant, or wherever I happen to be, I find myself sifting the faces around me. Once, I followed a man in seersucker for blocks, only to discover he bore not the slightest resemblance to my man.

I am beginning to think I'll never see him again when I spot him, one evening, coming out of a theater. He's tanned and appears to be in much better circumstances than he was the last time I saw him. A very tall, not very young woman is with him. She stands off to one side while we talk. He asks about the lawn, how it's coming.

"It isn't."

His smile fades. "You're kidding me?"

"No. It's a total flop. I've given up on it."

"You used the fertilizer and . . ."

"Everything. I did everything you said."

He seems genuinely concerned, but I realize, after a minute, it is no longer the lawn he is talking about. It's Jules.

I don't remember ever mentioning the boy to him. Yet he knows. He knows. I have questions, but none of them really educes the answers I am looking for. It's frustrating, and now the woman is at his shoulder, muttering something to him. The man's expression never changes, makes no concession whatever to what the woman is saying to him. She moves off again, moves even farther away from us this time.

"No improvement at all?" he asks at last, though I am not sure now whether it's Jules or the lawn he's referring to.

"None" is my answer to either of them.

He says he doesn't understand it, and follows the woman, who is now getting into a taxi. He is going slowly, pauses to ask me how long it's been.

"For which one?"

He turns to me, gives me a thorough look before saying that he wished we had more time. I have the same wish, but I don't think he hears me. He's already bending into the cab. I repeat my wish. The door slams, and I am left looking long after them.

Jules will not say whether or not he knows the man. He says he won't discuss anything with me until I begin to take him seriously. I always thought I had, I tell him, and ask if he can't be more specific. He says he can, but doesn't care to.

"You're making it impossible for me."

He peers at me through this crack he has allowed the door, peers at me and says finally that he has been told he has a lisp.

"But you don't drive a Hudson."

It was a joke, a bad joke, I add almost immediately, but the door is already closing between us.

The lawn appears to be coming around. The weeds have been checked, and even Edna's mother (visiting with us) remarks on the color. Vibrant is the word she uses. I am in the process of getting her bags. She was to have stayed the week, but Jules proved a bit too much for her. She took his retreat personally, got it into her head that she had somehow produced it. We couldn't convince her otherwise.

Edna hasn't given up. She's joined us on the steps. I immediately leave them to take the bags to the car, and watch from there. Edna is fooling with her hair, has this imperiled look she sometimes gets. I turn away at this point, and I am genuinely surprised, a few minutes later, to see Edna's mother approaching the car alone. Edna has not moved from the steps, where, it seems to me, she is still talking.

I drop Edna's mother at the station and, heading back by way of the parkway, think I spot the Hudson. It goes by me so fast, I'm not even sure of the color. I follow the car to an exit long after mine, and an old Victorian house, watch it pull into a dirt driveway. The color and year are right, but the man isn't. He's a small man, blond and too young. I wait for him to go inside, then copy the names (there are two) on the mailbox. Someone is watching me from an upper window, I realize, as I start back to my car.

Edna is feeding the cat when I get home. She doesn't ask what kept me. I tell her anyway. I tell her about the Hudson, about following it all the way out to Patchogue. She interrupts me.

"I want him down."

I hesitate, thinking I may have misunderstood. I haven't, it becomes clear, though I still don't know that I have anything more to say. She is still squatting there, doing whatever it is she is doing with the cat, but her eyes are on me and I can see that she means business.

"It's been one hell of a day, hasn't it?"

Her look darkens.

"We could do the thing with the food. You know, not bring it up to him anymore."

She does not quote suicide rates to me this time. There is nothing from her but the cat, protruding now between her legs.

"You want me to? You want me to tell him we won't be bringing it up to him anymore?"

She doesn't care, she says, going for a tuft of hair at her neck. I take the hand with the hair in mine. She slips her hand away at once, and I go upstairs to tell Jules. He laughs and, with an exaggerated lisp, tells me what I can do with my food.

Knowing him, I give Jules until breakfast. Lunch at the latest. We used to rib him about his appetite. He can put away vast quantities of food and, within the hour, complain of hunger. He's just thirteen and already the size of his brother, Lawrence, in his first year at Cornell. Once, fooling around, I challenged him to an arm wrestle. We must have been at it a good five minutes before I finally wore him down. He was in tears, I remember, and swore it would be different the next time.

He's gotten through breakfast. And I'm told by Beth (my daughter) the instant I walk through the door this evening that he didn't come down to lunch, either. Beth is not quite ten, and takes an extremely clinical view of her brother's predicament. Her question, for example, the moment we sit down to dinner, much later than usual, is how long a person can go without food or water.

"Much longer than you think," I reply quickly, and add that Jules has certainly been drinking.

"How do you know?"

"I simply do."

Edna turns to me and, when I have nothing further to say, back to the stairs. I say something then, but it is too late and not really pertinent.

"Even if he is drinking," Beth continues, "how long can he go?"

I warn Beth that if she persists along these lines she'll be asked to leave the table.

"What did I say?"

Edna asks us both to be still. We are, at least for the minute. The child then declares that it is impossible to live under such conditions and noisily removes herself from the room. I try to joke about it, but it is clear that Edna is weakening. He can't hold out much longer, I assure her.

"Neither can I."

"You're doing fine."

"I'm shitting in my pants."

"Fine. You're doing fine."

"We're losing him."

The laugh I want does not come. What does come is a sort of whine. I go to her, bang my hip on the edge of the table.

"What did you say?"

"My hip. I hurt my hip."

"I thought you said something."

Her head is in line with my stomach. I have only to tilt her slightly for her head to rest there, but I don't. I don't touch her. I promise her he'll be down, down for breakfast, I promise her.

He's not. Edna has laid a place for him, is again warming his food. Mine lies cold and intact in front of me. A coarse sunbeam slants across the top third of my plate, a portion of my hand. The hand looks severed. If I sit here any longer, Edna says, I'll miss my train.

I call Patchogue information once I get to the office and learn that only one of the names I copied from the mailbox is listed.

The name is Lewis, and I can't reach them. I must have tried twenty times throughout the day, and at least twice since I've been home. I'm just putting the phone down, in fact, as Beth walks in. She wants to know who I was calling. I can honestly tell her I don't know.

"It makes no sense."

I agree.

She eyes me suspiciously, abruptly shifts the subject to her brother. She thinks he might be coming down to the kitchen while we're asleep.

"You're all heart, Beth."

"I'm not fooling."

"What do you want me to do, put a lock on his door?"

"No, on the refrigerator."

I finally get through to this Lewis in Patchogue. The minute I hear the voice I realize I have the wrong man. The Hudson (my reason for the call) belongs to his brother-in-law and, so far as he knows, is not for sale. That's as much as I can get out of him. He won't even let me have the man's number. I leave mine, ask that he be sure to have his brother-in-law get back to me. "Anytime," I add, and wish I hadn't. It sounds too much like a plea. In any case, I can, if nothing else, assume the other name on the mailbox (Chambers) to be the brother-in-law's and, it occurs to me, Edna might be familiar with it.

She isn't. She does know a Chalmers whose child, she recalls, used to get along well with Jules. "They were about the same age, and I remember how upset Jules was when they moved. New Brunswick, I believe it was. Maybe I ought to give them a call . . ."

She's twisting her hair, and I'm getting angry. I'm very angry. I race upstairs and demand that Jules open his door. He'll open it, he says finally, only after I bring him a tuna-fish sandwich.

"I'm warning you."

"On rye."

"I'll break the door down."

"Go ahead."

"Who's Chambers?"

"Break it down. Go ahead, break it. I'd like to see you do it."

I can't. I want to, but I can't. I don't have the strength, and my shoulder gives out on me. I think I may have dislocated it.

"Go on, break it down. What are you waiting for?"

Half an hour later, I can't even raise the arm. While I'm soaking it (no one tells me at the time), Chambers calls. Edna says she didn't want to disturb me. She thought she was doing me a favor, and says she doesn't understand why I'm getting so worked up over some used-car salesman.

"He's not a used-car salesman."

"What is he?"

"I'm not sure."

Her jaw slips, and the look is derisive.

"I don't know him. Not really."

"I feel the same way about you sometimes. You never even mentioned you were considering another car."

"I'm not."

The look is impatient now. I try to explain it to her, but it doesn't even make sense to me, and presently I simply stop talking.

My shoulder keeps me up half the night. When I do fall asleep I dream a fragmented dream. Once, I am in a large open space, a field maybe. And immediately I am transferred to a narrow, cramped place which I come to understand is a refrigerator and that I am not alone in it. Jules is there. He's large, larger than I am, and he's eating. He's eating, and somehow, the more he eats, the smaller I get. It's me he's eating, I realize. And I don't mind. I welcome it, in fact. The smaller I get, the less cramped I am, the more comfortable it is.

Edna says I was moaning all night. She thinks it was my shoulder. The shoulder is sore, so sore I have to hold my fork in the other hand. It's slowing me down, and Edna, for the second time, reminds me that I have a train to catch. She's moving around me, moving quickly around me from one spot to another. Her elbows, I notice, have a very old look to them. They are the only sign of age, of anything, it seems to me, having passed between us. And I find myself drawn, drawn in a way I didn't think I could be anymore, into those dark, wizened regions of hers. I reach out for them, forgetting my shoulder, and never hear the phone. The pain travels straight to my eyes.

"It's him," she whispers, a palm cupping the mouthpiece. "I'll tell him you left."

I motion for the phone.

"You'll miss your train."

I take the phone from her. With his first words the pain goes. My problem is introducing myself. He doesn't seem to remember. I mention the station, his help with the lawn. I am talking about the lawn, how well it turned out, when I notice Edna preparing a tray. I ask her to wait.

"For what?" she replies, so loudly that Chambers asks what's going on.

"Nothing," I answer, and return to what I had been saying about the lawn. "Marvelous, really. It worked out just the way you said it would. I had my doubts, I want you to know. I was doubting right up to the time I ran into you at the theater."

"I thought you said it was the station."

"This was another time. You were with this tall, very attractive woman."

"You have me mixed up with somebody else."

"That's exactly what I thought when you first approached me."

"I approached you? Why would I approach you?"

I hesitate here, and he says I've definitely got the wrong man. "I don't go in for that sort of thing."

I have to laugh, and he calls me an animal, a fucking animal. "All this bullshit about being interested in the car."

I admit it wasn't the car I was after, but before I can explain further, he's hung up on me.

The phone is whining. It is still in my hand, Edna points out, and that I am blocking her path. She can't get by, she repeats, as I try to tell her what went on between me and the man. She doesn't want to hear about it. She wants me out of her way. I try, but she is suddenly going in the direction I am, and we collide. She loses control of the tray. Its contents fall between us. I seem to have gotten the worst of it. I look at her and smile. Pure slapstick, I say. And it is. It's some idiotic joke we're involved in. Me sloshing around in maple syrup, she with a piece of bacon clinging somehow to a breast. It's a laugh. You have to laugh about it. And I am, I'm laughing, laughing uncontrollably by the time she walks out of the kitchen.

I clean up the mess, phone my office, then go up to talk to her. It's no use. She cries, says things, things that even at our worst she's never said to me. Then she becomes quiet, very quiet, and soon, without looking up at me, asks me to go.

Somewhat of a haze has developed, but it is still a fine day. I prune the azalea I've been meaning to for so long; then I go in, make some tuna-fish sandwiches, and take them up to him. **Q**

Greving

For six days and nights now it has been raining, a small August rain, bouncing on the roof of the tent. Evenings, you can hear the water sliding from the leaves of those twisted trees that run down to the river, and when it is late, the elephants come to drink. At breakfast, the men who work the mess say this can't be, that there are no elephants in the area, but they tell us, too, that the rains will stop. Still, Brand has seen the elephants, through the screened half-moon windows that let in the air at night. Often, when we are lying on the cots, quiet and ready for sleep, Brand will get up and walk to the windows to look out. Crossing the floor, bare feet on common wood, his eyes shining in the dark, he makes less sound than the rain that falls on the roof. As if he were vanishing, except that I can see him framed against the slit of sky, head to one side, waiting. Sometimes he will stand there, motionless, for twenty minutes or more before returning to bed. It is not that he cares about the elephants. But they have become a kind of comfort, something to look forward to at the end of these days that seem never to end, and they do not disturb us.

Perhaps Brand is vanishing, but at least there is very little to disturb us here. Our tent perches just above the brackish waters of the river which circles the camp on three sides. Across the river, you can see the plains, high grasses waving when the wind is full, heavy-topped trees scattered in the distance, a gray sky beyond. Sometimes, too, you can see the herds of kudu hemming their way along the horizon, although they are less conspicuous than one might have expected. It is a used-up landscape, a place in which nothing more can happen, and yet, it cannot be ignored. To the fourth side of the camp runs a high electric fence that, like the river, keeps the animals out, but still, the baboons occasionally get into the mess tent. Then the cook chases them, screaming in Swahili, waving a wooden spoon, and he usually has his way with them. Besides the cook, two other caretakers, and Modest, who drives the jeep, we are the only people at the camp, except for an English couple on holiday with their daughter, and she is well behaved. The five of us have everything we need—clean towels each day, enough drinking water, mosquito netting, jeeps with fairly new tires should the weather clear. Each week a Piper Cub arrives with fresh supplies—it will arrive tomorrow afternoon again—so there is always enough to eat. The food is quite acceptable here, and the bar stays open until we are in bed.

Brand and I have also brought a good deal of our own equipment—maps, compasses, gum boots, a deck of cards, canteens, a butane stove, a penknife, sunscreen, sunglasses, sleeping bags, Cutter's, plastic bags, a tripod, a small telescope, a box of Cheez-Its, and Band-Aids. We are prepared to stay here a long time, if need be, and longer. Even so, Brand says that the early hours, before the rains begin again, fall harder and harder as the days go on. That is all he says, but I know what he means, as if everything were possible but unlikely—birds flying south in reddish light, or the elephants who drink in the night, or more simply, the way someone may look when reading in bed by the lamplight. I keep telling him that this has happened because we are south of the equator, but he says no, it is the climate, and no doubt he is right. We were happier in Nairobi, before the rains had come, and we were still in earnest about the facts.

I do not think I would mind the rains were it not for the greves, which are very difficult to look for in the rain. For all we know, they are land birds that have nothing to do with the water, although people frequently confuse them with loons. It is a common error, based on the general shape and the fact that in both species most pairs are solitary, as anyone versed in these matters will tell you. Even I know this, because Brand once told me, just as he keeps telling me that the rains will end, if not sooner, later. It was possible, even today, because at dawn the sky streaked light in silvers and grays, worn stone-smooth and polished. The jeep tracks have gotten very muddy in the last week, but still, we took an early run toward the mountains in the south, and Modest gloated cheerfully over our possibilities. Where he comes from, near Kisumu on the lake, the weather is rarely poor, or so he says. Modest is a fine driver, although from time to time he steers us into a ditch and we have to walk back to camp to fetch a rope. Still, he is always cheerful, which scandalizes the English couple when he takes them tea in the afternoons. It is in his nature. This morning he suggested we skirt the grasses along the river to look for crocodiles. Often people come to Africa just to see a crocodile, or to shoot one, but if they do not have a cunning guide, they may miss their chance. Crocodiles are Modest's specialty, and he is not bad on lions, either. But he knows nothing about the greves, not even that they rarely nest near rivers. Still, it makes little difference, since before we had gotten far enough along, the clouds had gathered and broken open again and we had to return to camp. This put Brand in the foulest of moods. He did not eat lunch and spent the rest of the day in the tent, dismantling and reassembling the binoculars we had bought on the coast, a Japanese pair. When I went in to see if he would have a game of hearts or two, he did not even look up, just kept screwing the opticals left and right, right and left, and adjusting the focal planes. At twenty-three, he still has the hands of a child, moist as if from sleep, although I know he has not been sleeping much. It has been like that for almost a week now.

Perhaps that makes little difference, either, since Brand speaks hardly at all these days and often takes to the tent. He says it's fatigue. But in truth, I am growing skeptical of his passion for the greves, although we have come all the way to Africa for no other reason than to find them. I do not know which of us first insisted on the trip or how we were sure the greves could be found. In fact, I cannot even say when we first knew about the greves at all. Perhaps they were simply a reason to come to Africa, an outgrowth of our ABC's, stories told one summer after evening had gotten on. Then again, the greves may have occurred on their own, but who is to say which of us conceived this passion in the first place, or when it took flight? Still, that we had reached an unspoken agreement of purpose cannot be doubted. It gave us, if not a life here, at least an itinerary, a receding point toward which we traveled. But that was before the rains, maybe even before we arrived at this camp.

It must be admitted that there was a time when we thought of nothing but the greves. We discussed them daily, considered their flight patterns, made detailed sketches in several colors. Their feet are always webbed, their tails cropped, and, as my drawings indicate, I think that their heads have human shape. In point of fact, the resemblance may not be entirely accurate, but in theory I am correct.

Out here at the camp, though, it is hard sometimes to remember even the recent past, say, that first morning back in Nairobi, when, long before I was up, he had already gone down to breakfast. Brand always eats breakfast, on principle, even when he is not hungry, although this has changed since we arrived at the camp. I found him at the terrace bar, where the barman was wiping glasses and chatting nervously with two ladies from Brighton. Brand may have eyed them in a composed way, like Robert Browning at a tea party, except that he was wearing shades and drinking pink gin. *Chin chin* and good morning, he would say, and how does mademoiselle find our gracious city? We have a population of 818,000, mostly Indian and black, and the rains don't come till September. The clubs open at ten, close at four, and William Holden can be reached at the Norfolk. Brand could be counted upon to say such things, at least before we reached the camp.

If I tell him we are at the Norfolk, he won't seem to hear,

PAMELA SCHIRMEISTER

and off he will go with the facts. I do not know how Brand knew so much about the city, or how he thought to order pink gin, but then, he is always full of facts and believes in keeping off the malaria. He can tell you the heights of mountains and the lengths of rivers, and who betrayed whom in the Wars of the Roses, and how the greves nest. He has known these things since he was a child. He also knows several words in Swahili, which I have heard him use around the camp. He ordered me a gin in English.

At that time, of course, we did not know about the rains, and I still believed in Brand's command of fact. I believed in many things. Besides, Brand always goes about a project with the utmost caution. He will not be hurried. For this reason, we spent two blissful days trying on cheap safari clothes. Brand bought several shirts and a canvas hat, which he wears pushed forward and tilted left, with a pencil stuck in the band. Brand often buys a hat wherever he goes, also on principle, although he refuses to say so. We then spent a lot of hours unsuccessfully ransacking the local bookshops for a copy of Aristotle's *Poetics.* There was something I needed to check on, although now it escapes me. Instead, Brand found three copies of *Johnson's Guide to African Birds,* all of which he bought on a whim for sixteen shillings.

I was not opposed to the purchase, because in Africa it is necessary to have some reading material. If you have ever seen any of these books, you will know that the pictures in them are extensive and colorful. They come six to a page, with brief descriptions of appearance and habitat printed below. Each description is clear and vigorous and conveys the author's passion for his subject. It is hard to imagine a more appealing style of writing. At the back, charts indicate migration schedules—of condors and crows and starlings and shrikes, all of which is helpful, even if these guides do not include much information about the greves. None, in fact; but that is because the author was an imperfect naturalist.

Even so, for a while Brand read them every day with great

45

care and did not offer to let me see them. I know, though, that he had them on Mt. Kenya, where, after an attack of altitude sickness, he huddled against a boulder and read with fervor until his dizziness had passed. After that, he seemed to enjoy the prospects, and especially the sudden fog that rolled in somewhere around nine thousand feet, but finally, our climb was less than successful. I had tried to tell him that in these heights no greves would come, but he did not listen and muttered about a frozen leopard found near the top of Kilimanjaro. Neither would he hear of heading east to the coast before trudging across the plains and north through the Rift Valley. He carried the guides out there as well, through every village we visited, showing the pictures to chiefs and boys, mothers and daughters, attempting to pose questions while marking certain pages with pencil notations in his minuscule scrawl, just as when he writes a postcard to Mom or Dad. Brand is an obsessive writer of postcards. I doubt that if the cards arrive, anyone will be able to read them, although they will assume that our message is clear: *Having a good time, wish you . . .* Certainly no one suspects that the greves mark the limits of our African travels—the continent is large—not even I would have suspected as much. And yet now, with Brand as he is, only the greves remain. It is certain that any day we may see them, for on what other grounds could we still wake each gray morning to the value of what we say and do?

That is wrong to ask, since it is no longer a question. We do continue to wake, and I suppose everything would have gone according to the book had we held on to the field guides. But they have since been lost, even though Brand looked after them everywhere we went. I am sure he had them still on the coast, and maybe even out on the islands near Manda, where the airstrip is. But one night he simply went to bed, no turning of pages, no making of notes, no sitting far into the night, or any farther. Perhaps it was on the train to Malindi, perhaps he grew sullen and left the books in the compartment. I contacted the officials to see if we could get them back, but they could not help us. That was the day we bought the binoculars, on the theory that the greves might fly high enough so as to be beyond sight of the human eye. Since then, I have continued to use the binoculars daily—they are very powerful—but Brand has not been the same without the field guides.

That was twenty-four days ago, although it seems longer, and no longer may we be so free in our travels. We have been from north to south and back again, and now we are come on this camp as to a final place. I notice that Brand has been aging more perceptibly in these last weeks—the rains, I suppose, or maybe the sky. And yet he never watches the sky anymore in the small hours, which, we have long since suspected, is the likeliest time to see the greves. We will know them by the black bands on their wings; specula, they are called. We knew that at least several weeks ago. In fact, we knew everything before we arrived, even that certain species cannot walk. They hobble. On these grounds, the greves must be searched out in the air, caught in flight or not at all, since on land they would look much like ordinary birds; loons, as I have said.

There is even a species of water bird around the camp that resembles the greves. They waddle about the banks of the river and in and out between the tents. Brand watches them with extreme distaste, as if they impinged upon his sense of decency, and occasionally he throws small granite pebbles at them when they cross his path. It is not their fault that they upset him, and he ought to leave them alone. Besides, the protest is pointless, since several ordinary species may resemble the greves, which no doubt explains a possible mistake, back when we first arrived here. Crossing the camp toward the jeep, just before dawn, I saw a slow flock of dark-winged birds cut the sky. There may have been twelve or fifteen of them, flying close together but without formation. They appeared to dip and circle, as greves will, and at the edge of sight their wings might have been black-banded. You could hear their cries—low, long—and perhaps you could hear them beat the air in their labored flight. By the time I had undone the binoculars, though, they had drifted out of range, just beyond vision and toward the south, where the mountains are. I saw them no more that day.

Brand did not see them at all—he was still in the tent—and I did not tell him about it. One way or another, it could only have upset him. Everything seems to upset him these days, or perhaps it is nothing at all, or just the elephants disturbing his sleep. I cannot say. He finally mentioned one afternoon that he no longer believes the greves exist, and yet he cannot quite give them up. The possibility of their being exerts a constant reproach upon him, and each morning, after we have come from our run in the jeep, he spends hours looking at the sky, head thrown back in the canvas chair, where he sits under the fly of the tent while the rain falls around him. I don't know what he watches for, since lately it is his impression that the greves are flightless. That is the only point on which we have argued this whole month long. But the greves cannot be flightless, as surely Brand must know. He will get over it. What he needs is a dry spell, with clear days, and time in the sun. For the moment, however, we are just waiting for a reddish light, with those birds flying south, if that is where they go. They may go anywhere, or they may stay put, we have not decided.

In the meantime, I have given up arguing with Brand. When he asks me when we are going home, I tell him that I do not know. We have a great number of things left to do, although Brand says he feels used up. I do not want to tire him further, so now, in the afternoons, I tend to my own business —a stroll around the camp, an hour or two reading, a talk with the cook. Today he was in the best of spirits because of the arrival of the Piper Cub. It is due at three. The cook said he requested several sides of beef, curry powder, and a case of cocoa, all of which will no doubt show up in tonight's dinner. Brand is very fond of curried beef. After our chat, it was still raining, but I asked Modest if he was up to a run, anyway. He agreed in his cheerful way, and together we tried to convince Brand of the wisdom of our plan. Of course he would not hear of it, and we left him sitting in his canvas chair, throwing those pebbles toward the river.

Modest and I drove out through the gate of the electric fence and toward the mountains. They lie green on the horizon like hills, but I have heard that from the air they divide the plains as a mammoth spine, licked clean by wind and water, ancient. There is no life there, although one day I would like to see them at close range, perhaps after the rains have ended. On this day, however, we contented ourselves with the usual route, along the river and through the trees. As always, the kudu were hemming their way along the horizon. They give the impression, even at a distance, of great power and grace, horns framed against the sky in endless procession. Still, Modest tells me that the kudu are fewer and fewer, and that the government worries about their extinction. Now is the season of migration, so they seem plentiful, but soon the beasts will be gone. I do not think I would miss them, but still, I asked Modest to head toward them for a look.

On the way, the rain let up quite suddenly, with a big wind coming to blow us around, and then the sky deepened, as if to leave us room. Tonight there will be a ring around the moon. Modest grew more cheerful than ever, about crocodiles, about the English, about the kudu, but I told him that I did not care about the kudu anymore and wanted to get back to camp. The ride took about an hour, and all the while I was thinking of Brand, of his hands on the binoculars and his passion for the field guides, of the twenty-odd days we had been here, of how he would feel if the dangers had been diminished. The rains may be dwindling, and yet I am not sure that the dangers can be diminished. But then, it is not for me to say so to Brand. Or perhaps there are many things for me to say, but it is difficult to think clearly when you are being ridden ragged across the African plains in a jeep. Several times I urged Modest to pay less attention to the brakes and more to the ditches that ran at the sides of our track.

Finally, in four o'clock light, the camp came into view,

comforting, a reasonable amount of space on this continent, which, after all, is not so large. It is true that the greves have made Africa larger for us in ways we could not have foreseen. Nothing could have predicted the expansion that we feel. But at times it has been almost too much for us, and being at camp has helped us to fill the space, so that now we may remain. Once through the electric fence, I walked slowly around the mess, where the cook could be heard singsonging over his beef, past the tent where the English couple continued their holiday, past the clearing where Modest was wiping down the jeep. I thanked him for the ride and headed for our tent. Brand's coat was slung over the chair out front, drenched, and he had left the binoculars in pieces, lying on the cot. He was not there, so I walked back to the mess, but he was not there either, and when the cook emerged with his wooden spoon, he told me that Brand had taken the Piper Cub out at 3:15 and that we would be having curry at supper.

That was awhile ago, and soon it will be longer. The rains have not yet returned, which greatly increases the chances of spotting the greves, although no longer do the elephants come to drink at night, because the water in the river is low. Each day Modest and I go for a run, both morning and afternoon. I take pictures then, and in the evenings I go to bed early. There is more work than ever to be done on the greves now, and I need rest. But sometimes, late, when I am lying on the cot and a cool air comes through the screen, I think of the photographs we will have at home, pictures of a long prospect on the road out of Nairobi, or the mountains as seen from across the river, or maybe the sky above the camp in early blueness.

Brand is not the way he looks in a photograph. Even so, I can see him just before sleep, stretched out on the cot, boots on, hand dangling just above the floor. He does not move when I speak his name, or when I enter the tent. The light inside is failing now at afternoon, and overhead, you can hear the water running from the canvas roof. If I watch him for a moment, I remember his fingers curling as they hang above the floor, or maybe the curve of his chin against the pillow. His hat is resting lightly over his chest, rising and falling with his breath, and there might be an imperceptible smile washing across his mouth. **Q**

Juggernaut

When I was seventeen, Kirby and I had a teacher who was crazy. This happened in the last year before Houston got big and unlivable.

Big Ed, we called him: Eddie Odom. Mr. Odom. He taught geometry as an afterthought; his stories were what he got excited about. Class began at nine o'clock. By 9:20, he would be winded, tired of sines and cosines, and he would turn to the clock in a way that almost aroused sympathy—so tired!—and he would try to last his lecture out for another five or ten minutes before going into his stories. The thrill that Kirby and I felt when he lurched into these stories following a halfhearted geometry lecture—there would be no warning whatsoever, we would suddenly be listening to something as fantastically wild and free as geometry was boring, and we wouldn't have done anything to earn it, we'd find ourselves just pulled into it, in the middle of it, and enjoying.

He had lived in Walla Walla, Washington, for a while, he told us the first day we were in his class, and while there he had a pet lion and had to move back to Houston after the lion stabbed a child in the chest with its tail.

Houston, he told us, was the only town in the country that was zoned and ordinanced properly, so that a man could do what he wanted, as he wanted. He paused for about five minutes after he said this, and looked at us, one by one, going down the rows in alphabetical order, to make sure we had understood him.

Simmons, Simonini; Kirby and I watched him sweep down the aisles, student by student. There was a tic in his eyebrow that flared alarmingly when he passed over Laura DeCastagnola, who was tiny, olive-skinned, exuberant, and good-calved.

Possibly he was trying to be a hero for her. All the rest of us were.

Big Ed was graying, in his late forties, possibly even fifty, slope-shouldered, of medium height—literally taller than half of us, and shorter than the rest—and he moved with an awkward power: as if perhaps once he had had this very great strength that had somehow been taken away: an injury inside, to some set of nerves, which still retained the strength but did not allow him to use it. Like a loaded pistol, or a car parked on the hill without an emergency brake: that was the impression he gave Kirby and me.

The child in Washington had been a punk, he told us, ten years old and foul-mouthed, but had lived anyway.

"All female lions have a claw hidden in their tail," said Big Ed—and then stopped and locked the whole class with a look, as if the last thing he would ever have expected was snickers and laughs. "No, it's true."

Kirby and I listened raptly: it was only the rest of the class which was disgusted by his callousness. Kirby and I were willing to give him that doubt. It was then, and is today still, our major fault. Nothing will get you into trouble so deep or as sad as faith.

While the rest of the class hesitated, froze, and drew back from Big Ed—not understanding, but reacting, an instinct they felt—Kirby and I ignored it, this avoidance instinct, shy of it, that growing-up spring, and plunged after, and into, his stories. We didn't look left or right. No one could be that crazy. Besides, we were frightened of growing up.

The point of the story had to be that female lions had claws in their tails. The other was all a smoke screen. No one *truly* believed a ten-year-old boy deserved to be stabbed by a lion.

He encouraged us to go down to the zoo and somehow manage to slip a hand in through the bars of the lion cage, behind them, and find out.

"It's hidden, deep under all that fringe. It's as sharp as a nail, and like a stinger, only curved: just another claw. My guess is, it's left over from a time we don't know about, when lions used to swing from the trees, like monkeys."

Feet would shift and books would be closed or moved around when the talk edged toward the ludicrous, as it often did.

The more adultbound of the class would even sigh, and look out the window—it was harsh spring, and green, the lawn mowers clugging thick and choking every few yards with rich wet dark grass, and its smell of fermentation—and we all had cars, that spring, as it was Houston, and Texas, and there weren't any of us who weren't handsome, or beautiful, or going places, or popular, or sure of it all. Except Kirby and me. And Big Ed would stop, slowly but also too, somehow, boltlike —that nerve again, perhaps—his eyebrows were arched and furry, and went all the way across—and he would squint his eyes at Cam Janse, shock-white bleach-haired and lanky, sunglasses, or at Tucker White, whose lips were big and curved, like a girl's, and who *had* all the girls—who would be pretending with these adult sighs and glances out the window that they would both be glad when the discussion got back to the more interesting topic of geometry—and so then Big Ed would assign about two or three hundred problems, about things we'd not even learned yet.

When the bell would ring, the boys sitting behind and next to Laura DeCastagnola were slower getting out of their desks than the rest of the class, and they walked oddly, holding their books at a ridiculous angle, close in and below their waists, as if aching from an unseen cramp. She had a jawline that you wanted to trace with your fingers. There was never a flatter, smoother region of face than that below her intelligent cheekbones. She made A's, and she was nice, and quiet, but she laughed like a monkey.

She would explode with her laughs, giggling and choking on them. She wore her cheerleader's dress on Friday. The blouse white without sleeves, the skirt gold. There were white socks. She wasn't sweet on anybody. She was everybody's sister. When she went to the football games and cheered, she was unique, standing under that vamp of mercury-haze gold twinkling light—a huge vacuum cleaner could have sucked it and all of its charged magic away, leaving us only under a night sky out in the Texas prairie—unique in that she was always conscious of the score and cared that we won, more so than about the party afterward.

"Go, *Ken!*" she would scream. Ken Sims, breaking free, getting to the sideline and racing down it in his gallop, running all wrong, feet getting tangled up, no forward body lean, a white farmboy from Arkansas, the leading scorer in the city that year. Calves like birds' legs. If Laura *had* had a boyfriend, it would have been Ken.

We'd see Big Ed, too, up in the stands, with his scarecrow wife, who looked to be ten or fifteen years older than he was, and was seven feet tall, with one of those small buglike dark rubies in the center of her forehead, though she was not Pakistani but pale, looked as pale and American as Wichita, or Fort Dodge. Big Ed would be watching Laura as if there were no one else down there, and while the rest of the stadium was jumping up and down, moving, orchestrating to Laura's leaps —her back to us when Ken was running—Big Ed would be standing there, as motionless as a totem.

I would nudge Kirby and point, secretly, up to Big Ed— his eyes would be riveted on her, his mouth slightly open, as if he was about to say something—and we would stop watching the game for a second and be troubled by it. We didn't see how he could be thinking it: lusting after a student, and such a nice one.

And down on the field, Ken or Mark or Amos would score. Our band would play that brassy little elephant song. And Laura would leap, and kick, and throw her arms up and out. We were on our way to an undefeated season that senior year. Who would want to lose any games in their last year? So we didn't. And we thought we were ready for that step, going out into the real world, and beyond.

It was such a time of richness that there was more than one hockey team, even—the struggling Aeros weren't enough. They played in the Spectrum, and were nothing more than an oddity—like so much else in the town at that time—and destined for a short life. The only reason people went to see them was that Gordie Howe, the Canadian legend, was making a comeback at the age of forty-eight and was both playing for and managing the team, and his two sons were playing for the Aeros with him, and he was scoring goals and winning games.

But there was another team, too, one that no one knew about, a seedier, underground version of the Aeros, and they played far out on the west end of town, on the warped and ratty ice rink in Houston. It was out on the highway that led into the rice fields, and tickets to the game were only fifty cents. The name of the team was the Juggernauts, and they played anybody.

We were driving then, had been for a year. We were free. Kirby had a sandy blue Mercury, one of the old Detroit iron horses from the sixties that would throw you into its back seat if you accelerated hard; and we would, on Tuesdays and Thursdays, race out into the night, away from the city's suburban lights, and pay with pennies, dimes, and nickels—for Kirby and I had vowed never to work—and we would grip our tickets and step through the low doorway and go down the steps and into all the light, to see the Juggernauts, on the arena that served as a children's skating rink in the day.

When we got there, the Juggernauts would still be out on the ice, down on their hands and knees, with thick marking crayons such as the ones used to label timber in the woods, and they would be crudely marking the hexagrams and baffling limits and boundaries of their strange game. I have been to wrestling matches since that time, and that is what the hang of air was like, though the fans were quiet, and many wore ties and sat up straight, waiting: hands on their knees, even the women's legs spread slightly apart, as if judging equipment at an auction, or even animals.

The games were sometimes violent, and always fast. We could never get the hang of the rules, and for us the best part was before the game, when the players crawled around on their knees with their marking crayons, laboring to draw the colorful, crooked lines, already suited up and wearing the pads which would protect them.

On a good night there would be maybe thirty-five fans: girlfriends, wives, and then, too, the outcasts, spectators with nothing else to do. There were people there who had probably driven from Galveston, just for the nothing event. The few cars scattered around in the huge parking lot outside nearly all had license plates with different colors. Most of the players were from Pennsylvania and New Jersey, even beyond. It seemed odd to play the sport in the springtime, as they did.

Everyone got their Cokes for free at the games. The players didn't get any percentage of the gate, and they didn't even get to play for free but instead had to pay the Farmer's Market a certain fee just to keep the lights on and the ice frozen; they paid for that chance to keep playing a game that perhaps they should have been slowing down in, or even stopping.

None of the Juggernauts wanted to stop! You could hear them hitting the boards, the sides of the walls, when they slammed into them. They skated so hard and so fast! It was hypnotic, and you felt you could watch it forever.

Ed Odom drove a forest-green Corvette to school, the old kind from the sixties—older even than Kirby's—and he didn't park in the faculty lot but, rather, on the other side of the concrete dividing posts, on the students' side, and he would arrive early in the mornings—steamy already, the sun rising above the apartment buildings and convenience stores, turning the haze to a warm drip that had you sweating even before you got to your locker—and he would cruise, so slowly, with the windows down, one arm hanging out, around and around the school, two times, three. Everyone saw him, and he saw everyone, and would nod vaguely, a smile that looked just past and to the side of a person, sliding away. He seemed to be like an athlete getting ready for an event.

In class, he would grow disdainful when the guys tried to ask him about his 'Vette: what it would do, how long he had had it, how much he had paid for it. He would look at some odd spot in the room—a trash can, or the place in the corner where the walls met the ceiling—and would seem disappointed in whoever had asked the question, almost frozen with the disappointment, if not of that, then of something—and he would seem to be unable to move: pinned down by a thing. His head would be cocked very slightly.

But one day he came to class looking like a thing from a Halloween movie: all cut up and abraded, bruises the color of melons and dark fruit, and a stupid expression on his normally wary face. His arm was in a sling. He looked as if the event had just happened and he had come straight in off the street to find a phone. There was blood soaked through his gauze. The girls gasped. He looked straight at Laura DeCastagnola, who looked a little more shocked and horrified, and also something else, than even the other girls—and even the guys, most of whom had no stuffing—even the guys looked away and were queasy, could not look straight at him. Kirby and I watched the class, and it seemed that Laura was the only one who could not take her eyes off him: one hand up to the side of her face, the way we all wanted to do, either in the dark or the light of day, while we whispered our promises eternal to her.

He sat down, slowly, without grimacing—focusing his mind somewhere else and far away to do so, it was easy to see —and we respected him forever for that—and he opened the geometry book and began to lecture.

Three days later, as the bruises began to wane and he moved more easily, he finally told us—but our concern had long passed, after his initial refusal to tell us, back when it had first happened, and we had grown churlish and lost curiosity,

and were merely disgusted at his childishness in holding back
the secret—all of us except Kirby and me, who were still hoping very much to find out. It was a thing that grew in us, rather
than fading away.

He had been driving down the highway, he said, and had
opened the door to empty his litterbag onto the highway—and
had leaned over too far and had rolled out. His wife had been
with him, and she had reached over with her long left leg and
arm, and driven away, after he fell out.

"I bounced," he said, "like a basketball. While I was
bouncing, and holding my ribs to keep them from breaking,
I counted." He paused and looked intelligent, as if he had
trapped us in a game of chess, but by now it was agreed on,
as if we had a pact, not to give him pleasure, and no one asked
him and he had to volunteer it.

"I bounced," he said clearly, enunciating quietly and with
his teeth—it was as if the words were an ice-cream cone and
he was eating it slowly, on a hot day—"twenty-two times."

His wife, he said, drove to the next exit, went below the
overpass, and came back and got him. Helped him back in
the car.

We drove to the hockey games whenever we could.
They didn't start until nine o'clock. Obviously all the players
came home from work and ate supper first. The games lasted
until eleven, twelve o'clock. There were fights among the fans
sometimes, but rarely among the players, as in real hockey. I
think that the fact that they played among themselves, again
and again, too many dulling intrasquad games is what made
this different. Though, too, it could have been just the spring.
There weren't any wars, and there wasn't any racism, not in
our lives, and we weren't hungry. There weren't any demands.
Sometimes Kirby would pay for the tickets; sometimes I
would.

Sometimes there would be a team not from our area playing the Juggernauts: a northwest junior college's intramurals-

champion team, or another, leaner and more haggard traveling band of ruffians, hangers-on in the sport: a prison team
sometimes, or worse. On these occasions the Juggernauts
would rise from their rather smooth-skinned and sallow, good-
natured (though enthusiastic) boy's-school-type of play—
happy, energetic zips of the skates, long gliding sweeps of
mellowness on the ice, cradling the puck along and beaming
—happy to be playing—and on these invader nights, against
the teams down from Connecticut, from Idaho and Sioux
Falls, they would turn fierce, like the same boys now squab-
bling over a favorite girl. On these nights of the visitors, the
ticket prices rose to a dollar, and attendance would swell by
half.

There would even be someone there with a camera and
flash, a skinny youth with a press card, perhaps real but probably manufactured, and good equipment, and he would be
crouched low, moving around and around the rink like a spy
shooting pictures. And though there was no reason for a photographer to be there—the Juggernauts were in no league,
none of these teams were, there was no official record of wins
and losses—certainly no newspaper coverage—despite this,
the Juggernauts always played hardest and wildest when the
photographer was there. It could have been one of the player's
sons or even grandsons, but that did not matter.

They skated with their bellies in, those nights, bumped
into their opponents without apologies and knocked them to
the ice (or were knocked to the ice themselves), and charged
around on the ice with short savage chopping steps of their
skate blades, as if trying in their anger to mince or hash the
rink into a slush. Some of them would breathe through gritted
teeth and make low animal sounds.

The Juggernauts had a player we all called Larry Loop. He
wasn't their captain or anything—they were a band, not a team
—and Larry Loop was large and chesty, and he raced down the
ice in crunching little high-knee steps whether they were playing against ax murderers or a seminarian school. Friend or foe,

Larry Loop would *run* on his skates rather than actually using them, and could travel just as fast that way, as it was the way he had taught himself to skate, and it was a thing to watch. You could tell he was not from the North. You could tell he had not grown up with the game, but had discovered it, late in life. He was big, and the oldest man on the ice, gray-haired, tufts of it sticking out from behind his savage, painted goalie's mask— though he was not a goalie—and more often than not, when he bumped into people, they went over.

It was amazing, actually, how easily the people Larry Loop crashed into went over when he hit them. They were just like something spilled. I think now that he had this great tactician's eye for analyzing, and would time his approach and hits— running at this odd, never-balanced velocity—so that he always made contact when they were pretty severely off balance themselves: his victims nearly always seemed to be waving a leg high in the air, or grasping with both arms for useless sky, as they went over. And he would run a little farther, definitely pleased with himself, definitely smug, and then remember to turn back and look to see where the puck was, if it was still even in play.

He was called Larry Loop, we decided, because as he ran, he swung his stick high and around, above his head, in a looping, whipping, exuberant circle, like a lariat, like a child pretending, with one arm, to be a helicopter. We almost expected to see him lift off. When you were close to it, you could hear the whistling sound it made.

He would gallop down the ice, waving his stick, drawing penalties for it the whole way, and I think it helped wind him up for the impact. He was what is called in hockey a "goon," an enforcer type whose best contribution to the game is usually restricted to rattling the opposition's better players.

Except that, pretty often, Larry Loop would score goals, too. Again, perhaps, those strategian's eyes, theory and logic, because everything was all wrong, it shouldn't have been happening, he drew his stick back incorrectly and almost always shot improperly, off balance, but one thing the thirty or so of us had learned from watching him was that when he was open and did shoot on goal, it was probably going to go all the way in.

When he scored, he went wild. He would throw his stick down onto the ice and race off in the opposite direction, in that funny little stamping run, and throw his masked face back, up at the low ceiling, and beat on his chest with his heavy gloved hands and shout, "I am in *love!* I am in *love!*" It was funny, and it was frightening, too, to Kirby and me, like a visit to New York City for the first time, and we liked to believe that all the wildness and uncertainty and even danger in the world was contained there in that tiny skating rink, set so far out in the prairie, in the spring, heavy overhead blowers spinning inside to prevent the ice from melting. It was more ice than any of us had ever seen, that little arena, set so far out away from the rest of the town.

The wind coming across us, our faces, driving back into town—and it was town then and not yet city—it was as it had been on the way out to the game, only better, because there had been hope, going into the game, and it had not let us down. Larry Loop had been good, and wild.

The rules were confusing, but we liked to watch. There wasn't any danger of, say, one of the players going down with an injury while the rest of them crowded around him, until one of them looked up into the stands, directly at us, and motioned, or ordered, one of us to go down there and gill in: substitute. Those damn rules—not knowing what to do, and the panic such a thing would give us. It would be a horrible thing. We drove with the windows down, and felt as if we had escaped from something.

"When you are born," Big Ed said—and he turned and looked at the farthest side of the class, and crouched, as if expecting an attack—there was maybe one small snicker, though by now, this late in the spring, most of the class was

tired of his old gray-headed mock-youth—"the hospital, or
wherever it is you were born, records the sound of your voice."
He straightened up from his crouch and looked less wild, even
calm.

"They record your first cries, the squawls you make when
the doctor spanks you"—his eyes were looking at the floor,
drifting everywhere but over Laura—"and they register them
with the FBI."

He was lecturing now, not storytelling. "Because every
voice is like a set of fingerprints. They have special machines
that separate and classify every broken-down aspect of your
voice—and you can't disguise it, it's more unique than a set of
fingerprints, it'll give you away quicker than anything, on a
computer. Because those things in your voice that they pick up
on tape don't ever change, over your life."

He seemed to take, for once, a pleasure in the actual content of this story, rather than in just the telling of it. Regina
Carr, Laura's best friend but not a cheerleader, raised her
hand and asked him—and she had a deep, husky, odd sort of
voice, as if something was wrong with it, and was perhaps
hoping it *would* change with age—"What if you weren't born
in a hospital? Or were born in a tiny little country hospital,
where there wasn't even electricity, just a midwife?" Regina
was from Oklahoma and, if possible, nicer even than Laura.
Maybe because her voice was funny and off, but she went out
of her way to smile at you, not afraid that you might get a crush
on her, whereas Laura was shy and quick with her laughing
monkey flash of white teeth, as if afraid she might lead you on
into thinking something else. It was maybe like she already had
someone. But it wasn't Ken! Ken was always running: running,
sweating with the team. Scoring those goals.

"The FBI calls you," Big Ed said with certainty. "If they
don't have you on file, they just call you up, talk to you awhile
about some bogus sales offer—storm windows, insurance,
Japanese Bibles—and then they hang up and they've
got you."

I dialed Kirby's number two days later and didn't say anything when he answered.

"Hello?" he said again. I hung up. But then the phone rang, and this time it was my turn to speak into the receiver —"Hello?"—and not get an answer.

We practiced changing our voices, talked like ducks, like old men, like street toughs to each other, practicing for when the FBI called and that moment was at hand. Tears of laughter rolled down our faces. We howled like hyenas. We could laugh at anything, and the pleasure of it was odd and sincere. Who would want to leave? If we couldn't date Laura and Regina, at least couldn't we be crazy, laughing, all the time?

One Thursday night Kirby and I went out to the game; the Juggernauts were playing the team of an insurance firm from Boston that was in Houston for a convention—there were perhaps a hundred or more people in the stands, on either side of the teams—and we saw that number 52, wild Larry Loop, had his mask off for once, and he was talking to some people in the stands; only something was wrong, he wasn't really Larry Loop at all, it was Big Ed, Ed Odom, our geometry teacher, dressed up like Larry.

He looked like a clown, the clown that he was, standing there in the bulk of Larry's uniform, ice white and heavy rich blue: again, like a little boy, playing astronaut, playing hockey player. He was wearing Larry's big mittens, and holding his stick, and hanging from his belt was the wild, frozen mask, a mute, noncommittal mouth cut into it for breathing. Big Ed was talking animatedly and, we could tell, intelligently about the sport, to a fan—a man in a business suit with a red tie and owl glasses, the tie swinging out away from him as he leaned against the glass to get closer to Larry Loop, to hear what he had to say.

We were howling again, at the audacity of Big Ed's trick, at first, but even as we were registering that thought, we were taking note of the day he had come into class so battered, of the way he was now standing on the ice, in his skates, casually, and of how comfortable he appeared, talking, even while wearing the big suit.

We weren't even tempted to go down and speak to him. Like quail in tall grass, we settled down deep into the back of the crowd and watched, without standing up, him play the whole game.

And the Juggernauts lost, twelve to eleven, though Big Ed —Larry—scored several goals, and we wanted to stay for the other part we liked, at the end, where the losing team—all sweaty and sore and exhausted—had to crawl around on the ice with rags, erasing the smeared and dulled blue-and-red stripes and boundary lines they had just put down hours before—they had to have it clean again, by morning, no sign that they had been out there and had had glory—and the Juggernauts, or whoever lost, would be crawling on the ice, wiping off the stripes, and grown men in hockey suits would be skating around with brooms, sweeping the ice smooth again—and it was a thing we liked to watch, and often did, but the crowd was gone this night, we were almost the only two left in there, and the arena wasn't the same anymore; it was as threatening as a dark, slow lightning storm moving toward us, and we had to get out of there.

Walking out, across the parking lot, trying to laugh and howl at the lunacy of it but also not able to—recognizing, and being troubled by, the first signs of insincerity, in this paradox —we stopped when we realized we were passing a parked dark-green Corvette, and that Laura was standing by it, and she was holding his coat and tie in her arms, the clothes he had worn in class that day, and she had the keys in her hand, and she wasn't a girl, she wasn't even Laura, she was just some woman standing there, waiting for her man, with hopes and fears and other thoughts on her mind, a thousand other thoughts, she was just living, and it wasn't pretend.

The night was dark, without a moon, and she held our surprised looks. In two months she would be graduating, and what she was doing would be okay then, we suddenly realized, if it was ever okay, and for the first time we saw the thing in its immensity, and it was like coming around a bend or a trail in the woods and suddenly seeing the hugeness and emptiness of a great plowed pasture or field, when all one's life up to that point has been spent close to but never seeing a field of that size. It was so large that it was very clear to us that the whole rest of our lives would be spent in a field like that, crossing it, and the look Laura gave us was sweet and kind, but also wise, and was like an old familiar welcome.

This was back in those first days when Houston was clean and just growing, not yet beginning to die or get old. Houston was young then, too. You cannot imagine how smooth life was for you, if you were in high school, that one spring, when oil was $42 a barrel and everyone's father was employed by the petroleum industry, and a hero for finding oil when the Arabs wouldn't sell us any. Anything was possible. **Q**

Writers

George Collier sat at his desk. It was Sunday afternoon. He was eleven years old. George Collier put a piece of paper into his typewriter.

THE DAWN

A Poem
By George Collier

The dawn is over
I see the clover

Deeply dissatisfied with this effort, George Collier took the paper out and crumpled it up into a little ball and threw it in the wastebasket. He began anew.

THE DAWN

A Novel
By George Collier

My thoughts are filled with brooding
anguish as I contemplate in agony the

Uncertain as to how to continue, he sat perplexed.

brooding agony which I tragically suffer
in the chamber pots of my mind.

Chamber pots. No, not chamber pots, he thought. Chamber closets? As he sat in his brooding agony, his little sister, age four, came unsteadily into the room and asked her brother for her daily swimming lesson. With the grave air of responsibility and protectiveness often seen in older brothers, George

Collier resigned himself to this interruption of his labor, climbed down from his chair, and took his little sister by the hand.

George Collier was teaching his little sister how to dive. However, the pupil continued to revert to her previous method of immersion and proved unable to advance beyond that stage known as the belly flop, which she executed in a rather torturous, histrionic way unique to her.

Although it could not be said that the siblings found no cause for mirth in this, George Collier's basic attitude toward his sister was that of a mentor for a promising protégé, and so he conducted his lessons with gravity and perseverance.

Boldly stifling the hilarity which his little sister never failed to arouse in him, the mentor persisted in his attempts to help his wayward pupil.

Anne Collier dictated a letter to her mother.

Dear Mother,
George is swimming out very far into the bay, as he has learned how to swim very well, and I can tell that Grandmother loves him more than me.

Yesterday George said we should pick up driftwood on the shore because it would be noble. So we picked up all the driftwood on the shore, and I know that Grandmother is more proud of him than she is of me. But I know you are not, my mother.
Love,
the late Anne Collier

The appellation she unwittingly attached to her name, an expression she had seen in the newspaper, she used for the vague air of pathos it seemed to carry.

George Collier sat at his typewriter.

ODE TO MY FATHER

By George P. Collier

Thirty-six years ago today
A new twig was born on the family tree
And that twig grew into a branch
And now it has its own twigs
And today that branch is thirty-six years old
And his name is Claude Louis Collier
And he is married to Louise Brown Collier
And his children are George Palmer Collier
And Anne Isabelle Collier
And Stewart Palmer Collier
And

Uncertain as to how to continue (as there were no more children in the family), he fell into an artistic reverie.

And he is the leader of this family
And we look up to him as a great man
And he is very noble
And it would be noble if I wrote an ode
Because it is our duty to be noble
And

The nobility of it all began to make him feel somewhat uncertain, and he put on his baseball cap and went pensively out to the backyard to play.

Anne Collier dictated her daily letter to her mother.

Dear Mother,
     I wrote a poem because George said it would be noble.

     I had a little Christmas tree,
     It was so very little,

I sent it to the market
To buy a pound of fiddle.

It was so very green, my dear,
I ate a Fig Newton.

Love,
the late Anne Collier

Dear Mother,
I changed some of my poem to make it more
noble. Here it is.

I had a little Christmas tree,
It was so very noble,
I sent it to the market
To buy a pound of noble.

I ate a Fig Newton,
Because it was so noble.

Love,
the late Anne Collier

George Collier had taught his little sister to speak in initials, to save time. That is, instead of saying, "George, what
can I do? I don't have anything to do," she would say, "G.,
W.C.I.D.? I.D.H.A.T.D." This, George said, saved complaint
time.

George Collier was writing a book of essays, *History and Its
Heroes.* At the time, his hero was Ulysses S. Grant, and George
had personally given himself the middle name of Ulysses.
George Ulysses Collier. Thus he began his new tome.

History and Its Heroes

By George Ulysses Collier

Chapter I

Robert E. Lee

Robert E. Lee, so noble, so brave, facing North to ward off invaders. We all can learn from his great life. A hero, real, was he. There has no greater lived than Robert Edward Lee.

In her Desperate Bid to be as noble as her older brother, Anne Collier turned in her version later in the day.

History and Its Heroes

By the late Anne Collier

History has had many heroes. I found a butterfly. I asked my grandmother if I could call up Chester and ask him did he see my butterfly. She said I could but I said, What if he's not at home? But she said if he wasn't at home, then no one would answer. You mean he doesn't have a butler?

THE END

It is quite true, as I have noted previously, that the mind of a four-year-old finds it difficult to concentrate on one single subject.

Late in the summer, the parents of these "little monsters" arrived on separate trains from separate ports of embarkation. Q

Listening to Stravinsky

Last month they cut down three full-grown elms on our street. It took an hour and a half, and with ordinary brooms, they swept the twigs toward the tall, boxlike orange truck with its funneled chute angled into a huge engine that sucked in every last leaf and stick and mulched them. A half hour per tree. On the door of the truck was lettered the name of the manufacturer, WHISPER CHIPPER.

When I first heard the high, menacing buzz, I was washing dishes. It sounded like a chain saw, like a drill to my skull; I could feel its grinding, pulsing hum in my teeth. Our cat, Paris, his ears flat back, dashed into the kitchen, and I hurried out to reason with the person attacking our porch. An absurd act, if I really believed someone was so close and that I was going to go and find out about the mistake or ward them off with a soapy dish sponge. And then it turned out to be the city workers cutting down diseased elms.

I watched them hack the branches, feed them into the chute, where they were torn into chips and—zow zoop—no more disease and beetles, no more tree. Those seven men swept the street briskly and meticulously, just as if their mothers were coming to visit. They probably have to be thorough and neat because of the beetles.

I was relieved: that was one situation I didn't have to do anything about.

Even shopping malls are not safe, but they don't want you to know that. Your child can be stolen right from under your eyes. At one of the malls, Southdale or Rosedale, I think, a two-year-old blond girl disappeared. The police were notified and sealed the mall at the doors. They found the little girl in the washroom. This woman had taken her. She had scissors in her hand. She was cutting the child's hair. She had already dressed her in boy's clothes. All is not well.

Things are not going well between us, between Perry and me. I don't know when that started. Was it when I went back to college? Or before that, when Lila was born?

Maybe I should visit my sister in San Francisco. She'll know what to do. Sitting there in her immaculate house with her two curly-haired children and sipping a mineral water, she will say she never liked Perry and she never understood what I saw in him all these years. She'll tell me to get a divorce, and good riddance. She's probably right.

But I don't think she'd care for Val, either.

Perry is a librarian. People think that librarians are harmless and cerebral. Actually, he's natty and clever and maybe murderous. He wears silk bow ties and has his hair styled by a New York City–trained barber. And in our early days he used to make me laugh.

I didn't even know I wanted a divorce until I met Val a year ago. He was my instructor at the university. His name is really Valentine, but everyone calls him Val. Me too. Only in my rapturous daydreams is he Valentine of the strong thews, Valentine of the blue eyes, Valentine of the gentle visage, Valentine of the silver hair. He is open and light and large. Perry is small and dark and closed. It is ironic that Perry should be the one who is honest. "We need to examine the circumstances and see what we can salvage," Perry said when I told him.

Here is how I met Val. I am twenty-seven and he is forty-two. I was working on my bachelor's degree, as much to get away from the kids as to have the degree. I was majoring in English, which Perry thought was impractical if I wanted to have a career. What I wanted was to be a different person three hours a day, an adult, a non-mother. I love my babies, but they are not everything.

Val—Dr. O'Neill—was teaching the Milton class. I do not like Milton, because he is so unloving, so finally certain about the world and human behavior, and such a blind bully that he makes me intolerant of him.

I said this to Val after class last year. He smiled indulgently at me, thinking no doubt of the self-assurance and pomposity of callow youth, and invited me for coffee at the student center, but I had to pick up Nancy and Lila at day-care. After the next class, I invited him for coffee, but he had an appointment with his dean, whom he characterized with atypical hyperbole as having a diseased and knavish itch for power. Even though, as a student, I paid no special attention to academic bureaucracy and gossip, I wanted to be interested in what interested him. I listened and nodded knowingly. I was determined to prove to him that I was no ordinary student; not that I was extraordinary, just that I was not mediocre. Already I was trying to please him.

I am a timid person, so I am surprised that I asked him that second time and more surprised that I asked him yet again. I was flattered that someone listened to me, heard me, even if I thought he was overly kind in attending to a woman who was merely a dilettante, a drifter, an escapee from housework.

There were three of us; another woman, Clara Hopkins, stayed after class and decided to join us for coffee. She *loved* Milton, she said, her voice loud and smug.

I kept quiet.

Val didn't say anything.

She thought Milton was an inspiration to us all. Her brown hair fell in greasy strands about her round face. She was twenty or so and had bumpy skin and a dark down on her upper lip. Perhaps she wasn't quite so grotesque. Perhaps I resented her being there with Val, being a superfluous tenant in my world. And what can a person do about bumpy skin, anyway? She continued to spoon banana cream pie into her little circle of a mouth. "I love the notion of *felix culpa.* That a mistake, a sin, could be better than purity."

"More precisely," Val said, "it has to do with the joy that comes through the redemptive act that atones for the sin."

My cup clinked on the saucer. "I disagree with both of you. I don't think that joy can make up for pain. You grab what you can before the ride is up." That was pretty daring for me. I was being the riotous hedonist, the insatiate sybarite. Why did I wish to appear an advocate of debauchery, when even in our sex Perry and I pursued nothing more adventurous than the missionary position? Foolish, foolish woman. Perhaps I was trying to outrage Clara. She did knit her brow and glare at me.

Val cleared his throat (for effect?—which sounds more theatrical than he is) and cast a measuring glance at me and broke into a smile. "I would not have taken you to be such a voluptuary. Go for the gusto, hmmm?"

"Mock on, mock on, Voltaire," I said.

His wife has multiple sclerosis. Nobody knows what causes it; it is a "mysterious disease," which makes it sound romantic. There are theories about infection by a virus, or a deficiency of particular minerals or enzymes, or an allergic reaction. Nobody knows for sure. The sheaths of the nerve cells are destroyed and scarred. The hardened scar tissue cannot, of course, function as nervous tissue. Her body in the very act of repair was betraying her. She can just barely walk with the aid of a walker, which she thumps down ahead of her and leans on as she pulls forward her heavy, almost useless legs. The disease may soon claim her sight and speech, too. She is losing more and more control over her body even as, unknowingly, she controls more and more of our lives.

There are periods of partial recovery, followed by periods of progressively worsening symptoms, of greater paralysis. Val won't leave her. They have no children. I suppose she is, in a way, his child to care for. I happened to be watching from across the street when he wheeled her out of the grocery store, her lap and legs covered with a brown plaid blanket. That my rival should be such a shriveled token of flesh!

Later I asked him why he didn't go shopping by himself after getting a list from her. He shook his head at my obtuse question and explained that occasionally she wanted to go to the store she used to go to. She has had multiple sclerosis for ten years, and will have it for ten or twenty or thirty more yet.

So is that what I'm doing? Just waiting for his wife to die? What does that make me? A ghoul? One of those people who stop to stare at accidents or road kills? I don't like to think of myself that way, but I have to admit that if I could cause her to die in a wish, I'd do it. That makes me a murderer in my heart. I would not wish her pain, but I would wish her out of our lives. He won't divorce her while she's dying. He won't marry me. It occurs to me that we three (and maybe four, if I count Perry) are married by chains of love and disease.

My dilemma: Perry wants me to live with him, but I'm certain he doesn't love me. Val, who does love me (probably), doesn't want me to move in with him.

I hate my life, what I've become. Maybe I am a terrible person, what the nuns called a "reprobate." Perry would think so.

I wrote out a check for a hundred dollars to the Ethiopian Famine Relief. And then I didn't want to hear about it anymore, didn't want to see pictures of sticklike humans walking on dusty paths, of babies with insects buzzing around their mouths and eyes.

Perry's friend George used to say I was lucky when I had one of my moods. He's in a wheelchair. He caught polio when he was eleven. It's true that I've never suffered from polio or fought in a war or endured famine, but I'm not "lucky." Every one of those things may happen to me yet. I may yet be un-lucky. Already my marriage is foundering. Terrible things may lie ahead. I might be picked off by a sniper. I could be maimed in a car accident, made so ugly that even darling Val wouldn't want me.

I cannot imagine a life without my lover, although I'm living it now, and obviously I lived without him before I met him. Like the song, "I ache for him. It's fever love."

I do believe love makes people crazy, its immensity and danger and despair. I'm not being whimsical. There are all sorts of craziness, and love is one kind. I think someday the scientists will discover this for a fact. They will find a chemical in the blood that makes a sane person insane, that gives a person maniac desires. Last March, when I hadn't seen Val for thirteen days because the course was over, I waited for him in the rain outside the campus theater, so it would seem I bumped into him by chance. For half an hour, like a fool, pacing back and forth, dripping, my fingers red and cold, I was hoping to catch a glimpse of him.

My friend Winnie had been taking his class and mentioned that he'd recommended the Bergman movie on campus. I arrived late for the film after an evening class. For the fourth time, I was studying the poster with coming attractions on it. I had turned away from the door and was startled by his voice in back of me.

"Can I give you a lift home? Diane?"

"Oh, hello. Dr. O'Neill."

"Were you just in the theater? I didn't notice you."

"I've seen *Cries and Whispers* before."

"What did you think of it? Did you like the movie?"

"Sort of." I decided to be brazen. "All those quivering psyches and throbbing questions . . ." I shrugged.

"You're a tough one," he said with an amused, skeptical expression, as if he didn't wholly believe his comment. "Let me give you a ride home. You look cold. Where do you live? In town?"

"Thanks, I've got my own car, thanks." I wished I'd walked, so I could accept his offer.

"I see." He pulled on his gloves.

I didn't quite know what to do. "This drizzle is awful."

"Yes, it is."

"I hope it doesn't continue. It wasn't raining when I went to class."

"No, it started this evening."

"I think it's letting up a little."

"A little, yes," he said, politely examining the sky.

"For the past half hour it's been just a slight sprinkle."

"You've been out in the rain for a half hour? Out here?"

"I left my umbrella at home."

Questions passed across his face, but he didn't ask them. I sneezed.

"I feel responsible," he said, with more humor than remorse.

"I didn't catch the cold from you," I said rather sharply. A student's crush might have been droll to him, but not to the student. "You're absolved."

"My umbrella is big enough for two. I should walk you to your car."

"To ease your conscience?" I did not want to be a moral obligation.

"Something like that." He put up the umbrella and extended his bent arm for me.

I walked close beside him under the canopy of the umbrella, with the soft rain promising spring. The puddles beneath our feet reflected the neon lights around us and shimmered into iridescent ripples moved by the invisible wind.

To break the silence I said, "How's your dean?"

"My dean?"

"You said he craved power."

"Donald Webb, yes. He's been tamed. Still our dean, but now the president wants to replace him. Something I'm sure Webb never figured would happen. He used to say he didn't come here to make friends."

"What did he do?"

"Made some bad and hasty decisions. But you don't care to hear about this."

"Truly, I do. It's interesting, very interesting."

"That's courteous of you."

Was that sarcasm in his voice or awkwardness?

"This your car?"

We had stopped next to my Datsun. I nodded.

"Would you like to have a beer in the Rathskeller? Or do you have to get home?" His voice faltered. "You probably have exams to study for, papers to write."

"I'd like to," I said.

We saw each other often after that.

This was last March. I was not some sex-starved adolescent newly charged with hormones. I was a twenty-seven-year-old married woman with two children and a husband.

I'm coming to hate Perry, but I never feel hate for Val, even though he won't let me move in with him. Perry calls me crazy, says I will eventually come to my senses, says I'm lucky to have someone who'll forgive my sluttish behavior.

My neighbors tell me I should "go into" real estate, that I like people and would do well. They don't really know me if they say that. I only *appear* to like people. Inside I'm willful, greedy, inconsiderate, flighty, selfish, moody, and lecherous. When we were living together, Perry said all those things about me except the last. That one he said when he found out about Val.

That spring Perry got weirder and weirder. One time in May he stayed up past midnight making chocolate-chip cookies and brought a plate with two dozen of them stacked on it into my bedroom, the guest bedroom actually. I was sleeping there because I had the flu and could not bear to be touched. Perry wanted me to eat the cookies.

"I don't want any. I ache all over."

"I baked these for you."

"*You* eat them."

"I'm on a diet."

Perry is 140 pounds and 5′8″. I sighed. "Have you checked on the girls?"

"They're sound asleep. You ought to have some cookies."

"Sure, Perry. Leave them here."

"You need your strength. You're ill. Want me to fix you some soup? I could heat up a can of soup."

"No, I just want to rest."

"I'll go open a can of chicken soup."

"I told you I don't want any. Don't you listen? Doesn't anything get through that goddamn skull of yours? Are you crazy or what?" Without a word, he stalked out of the room, and I could hear him in the kitchen, washing dishes and clanking pans. In a childish fit, I spitefully whacked the rim of the plate, which was on the edge of the nightstand, overturning it and spilling the cookies on the shag rug.

Perry came in, ridiculously holding a tablespoon in his right hand as if he'd just finished stirring the pot. "Now look at what you've done."

"Stop shrieking. You'll wake the children."

"Shrieking? Am I shrieking?" He waved the spoon at me. "You're the one who should lower your voice."

Lila started to whimper in the next room. It wasn't a pained cry, just a fretful whine. "You've wakened her," I said, some malicious gladness in my voice.

"Why did you throw the plate down?"

"I didn't. The dish was on the corner of the stand." I sat up and swung my legs onto the floor. Lila was still crying rhythmically.

"You did," and his eyes were fierce and unsparing, like those of a murderous stranger.

It's difficult for me to remember exactly what happened next and in what order, but I think (and I must not sanctify my own behavior, for surely I contributed to the heat of the events) he tossed that stupid spoon at my bare feet on the floor. And then (I don't think it was before, although perhaps it was) I kicked the Melmac plate toward the baseboard, and at the same time, I gave Perry a shove. I told him I'd been seeing another man. He called me a lecherous slut. I wanted us to separate.

He caught my wrist, squeezed it, twisted it. We are not violent people, but we came close to it that time. He released my wrist with a downward shake and whispered, "You're crazy." He turned and left the room.

I said he was becoming weirder, but perhaps I'm the one. He says I'm crazy.

He's not a brute. He probably has all sorts of wonderful qualities. And when I married him I'm sure I loved him, although it's difficult for me to remember now. And I'm certain I'm coloring this, since it's one side of the story only, not a balanced report.

Maybe he's going crazy. I don't know. He says I'm the one. Maybe he's right. Maybe we're both right.

Can that happen to two people who know each other so well they both are infected by the same lunacy, a contagion we're both susceptible to by virtue of years of proximity?

There have been many episodes of mass hysteria. Surely twin hysteria is easier to buy. He says we're not getting a divorce, he won't permit it.

The other day I came home and found my Datsun with its right fender smashed in. Perry said he had borrowed the car and that he accidentally ran into a parking meter. I would have believed him except for what happened after that.

The following week he borrowed my car because his was at the mechanic's. I was climbing the stairs to the second floor when I heard tires squealing. I stopped on the landing. A current bored through to my bone marrow. Afraid of what I was going to see, I peered through the window curtain. Perry had pulled out of the driveway into the street and was turning the car in a semicircle, aiming its right fender at the stop sign across the street. He deliberately rammed into it. The sound of metal against metal was surprisingly soft and fleshy. I did not see the sign pole move. Suddenly it was at a drunken, tilted angle. Fear filled my mouth, hot and dry, cleaving to my palate and arching back to my throat.

That was what he wanted to do to me. I would be one of those people who are killed by an insane family member. I used to wonder how it was possible that the family didn't notice that the person was insane. They know. There just isn't anything to be done. They must wait for the death stroke.

That afternoon I moved in with my friend Winnie, who has an apartment across town. I did not tell Perry. I took my babies and two suitcases and our cat. Winnie thinks I should file for divorce. She has a small room with an extra couch. The girls and I sleep in there. I brought a sleeping bag. I'm not so fearful anymore.

Val judges me, I see it in his face. He does not altogether approve of me.

Behind those eyes, he thinks I'm an adulteress.

He denies it.

How can he? I *am* an adultress.

"I would do anything for you," I said. "I would kill. I would rob. I would . . . do anything."

"No one's asking you to kill." The lower part of his face stiffened; the long creases on either side of his mouth, which were dimples in his youth (I've seen photographs of him as a beautiful child), deepened.

He must've thought I was reproaching him for not divorcing his wife. Perhaps my extravagant protestations *were* a means of accusation. But he did not come back with reciprocal protestations. Was he intending to cut free, to cast me off, the biblical adulterous woman?

I so wanted his approval. Fickle, fallible woman. As if I could clothe myself in his smiles or eat his good opinion. Like an adolescent rebel, I shunted wisdom aside, clasped dark impossibility to me. I pretended I was in paradise. Would I behave thus when I was fifty? Would I flirt and entice, preen and simper and paint my face? Would I bathe in the passion and not estimate the cost, pay gladly in pain? I marvel that I was so prodigal, that I did not care what I spent, what I lost.

I thought Val was reckless, but he wasn't. It turns out that I was the reckless one. He was shot through with responsibility, morality, duty, decorum. He'd been raised Catholic. I was baptized a Catholic but confirmed a heathen, I told him. He didn't think that was funny. He had his lectures to prepare. Next week classes would start.

I had to share him not only with his wife but with his students as well. Never be the other woman, I said to Baby Lila on my knee.

Just once I wanted him to be swept off his feet, rash, irresponsible, foolish, wild. He supposed double adultery was wild enough. He had to drive his wife to the clinic in Rochester. "I'm tired," he said.

We didn't even make love before he left town.

In the morning, I took the kids to the babysitter. I was nervous, jumpy, perhaps because Val was away. I decided to walk to the grocery store, which is a half mile from Winnie's apartment. I bought a light shopping bag of groceries. Inexplicably, LOVE was printed in a flourish of red letters on the brown bag. Was the word cheap or was it a charm intended to evoke the magic?

Two blocks from the store, a large van was stopped at the corner. It was medium gray, with a high cab, a snub nose, and rounded ends; there were windows in the side panels, but the glass was of the type that would not let you see inside. It was a smooth gray beast with black window eyes. It waited at the stop sign an inordinately long time, and my anxiety returned. I finally crossed not in front of it but parallel to it, and it moved past me slowly, the engine whining. I took a deep breath and, when the van was gone, concentrated on the overarching elm trees, their high leaves trembling and whispering in the slight breeze. I shuddered. As I crossed the next street, to my right I saw the gray van outlined against the rosy morning sky. This time it sped down the road toward me as if to run me down. It screeched to a halt at the stop sign and proceeded past me.

The driver could have been lost, someone new in town

who got turned around or who was looking for a particular address. Or it could've been Perry. Or some stranger.

I walked quickly. There was nobody else on the street. My breath came rapidly. I crossed the third street from Winnie's apartment and saw the van to my left. It drove by as I reached the curb. Its horn blared.

Now my breath was like a jagged knife. I tried to quiet my rising panic. Perhaps the driver was making a square around this neighborhood to familiarize himself with the area. I could always run up to someone's door and tell them the van was following me. But it wasn't exactly following. It was making a circuit around me.

As I watched the van drive away, a teenage girl walked past me. I took incongruous comfort in that. I was not alone. I caught up to her, then passed her, listening for her footsteps in back of me. Nothing could happen if she was in back and saw everything.

The click of her footsteps diminished. I slowly swiveled around to see her blond head disappearing around a lilac bush that bordered an unpaved alley. And behind me, gaining on me, was the large gray van, sunlight glinting off its sleek, impervious surface.

But it didn't follow me. It rolled into the alley.

I walked the next block so fast I almost tripped. I was making myself hysterical, I said. If I believed the van was evil, I should've rushed into the alley to help the girl. If I thought it was harmless, then why was I nearly running?

From the right, the gray van rumbled through the intersection in front of me.

I did run the last block to Winnie's house. I hurried up the back steps, glancing behind to see if the van was still following. My hand shaking, I fitted the key into the lock and let myself in. I put down the groceries and walked on tiptoes into the living room to look through the front window. No traffic, no cars at all. I went to the front door for a different angle on the street. Coming toward the house was the gray van. But it hadn't seen which house I entered. It didn't know. I watched it through the window in the door. It couldn't see me, could it? I stepped back as it drove past. But there was a window to my left. Was I silhouetted against the light?

The next day I checked the newspaper. My breath was ragged, as if I'd been running. No violent assaults were reported. No special brutalities.

I wondered if it was Perry. I wondered if he'd figured out I was with Winnie.

That evening, as I was playing records Val had lent me, I was startled by the chime of the doorbell. Perry. He stood in the doorway, would not come in, vaguely threatening, vaguely penitent. He wants me and the kids to move back. I told him I'd think about it, although I have no such intention. The van was parked across the street under an elm tree. He said he rented the van because his car was being repaired.

Winnie tells me to get a lawyer. I'm going to do it. I'm going to do it tomorrow.

Val and I meet when his wife is at the hospital. He brings records over. The other day we were listening to *The Rite of Spring*. Val was explaining to me about harmony and dissonance, about resolution and shifting rhythmic patterns. His wife is pretty sick now, and Val and I get to see each other often. Because his neighbors might suspect, he comes to Winnie's apartment. Her neighbors don't care.

So we make love. That is something. A person shouldn't wish for everything.

People should be happy with what they've got. **Q**

Rosella, in Stages

[6]

Some guests on the porch had just returned from a hike to the falls. They were loud. Rosella, crouching, studied them from inside the hemlock hedge. One fancy lady had little moss bits on her shoes.

"What swells the heart is timelessness."

"I must disagree. Rather, it is purity in the here and now."

This city man wore clothes like a farmer would, and went out every morning to draw. Rosella had followed him to Ship Rock and seen him pee over the edge. And then right away after, Mama looked at her outside the kitchen, said, "Have you been eating pitch again, Rosella?" and smacked her hard.

Mama didn't like so many guests this time of year, and having to cook for them all because Molly was away with hectic fever. The foreign people wanted trout for breakfast every day.

Which Poppa said meant they weren't Jews, at least.

Getting out of the hedge meant torn stockings, so Rosella went in the barn to take them off. It was nice to kiss the horse. He gave back warm air out of big nostril holes and pushed with his head. Rosella buried her stockings and shoes in the oat bin. She would say a man from the woods had robbed her.

They were still loud on the porch. About the President's doctors in Buffalo saying he ought to pull through.

"No reason for a one of these anarchists to be on the loose."

"But how to discover each one? They are the most devious people."

"Czolgosz? Anyone with two z's in his name, lock him up."

Rosella picked up an interesting stone.

[19]

The cylinder slowed on the Edison machine, and Rosella turned the handle so they might hear the rest of "Jitney Elopement" at its proper speed. Caroline halved the distance between them on the divan and proffered on her snow-white hand a nugget of crystallized ginger.

"I am quite sure," said she, "that I have never had a more enjoyable Christmas."

All the guests but she had retired. Beech logs popped and settled in the fireplace.

Caroline looked searchingly at Rosella. "And I hope it is not out of my place to say how glad I am that what between us began as an agreeable acquaintance has, in these few days, grown into a warm, close friendship."

The song had ended, but Rosella, in flushed perplexity, did not lift the needle.

"It seems so sad to me that circumstances by morning must force us apart." Caroline's green eyes glistened in the flickering light. "Might I beg you now for one goodbye kiss as a token?"

Rosella stiffened when the tip of Caroline's tongue grazed her lips. She smelled ginger and melting wax.

"Oh, my darling," Caroline wailed, pulling desperately at the fastenings of her bodice. "I would face eternity for you."

[32]

After Sunday Mass they left the girls with Otto's mother and drove on out to where the hotel had been. It was a cool day, but clear, and the leaves were still green. They teased and held hands in the car until the road curled away from the water and steepened.

Daylilies had gone wild all over the char. Foundation lines were untraceable by eye.

"This was the dining hall," said Rosella, standing in burdock up to her knees.

Otto had a piece of melted glass, twisting it in his big knobbed hand like a pitcher feeling the seams of a baseball.

"You had to balance plates all the way up your arm," said Rosella.

Hair falling over her eyes was lank and wanted washing, the way everything wanted it—roasting pan, black skillet, walls and windows, the children when they filled their diapers, Otto when he came off a train: the day run to Albany, the two-day run to Utica.

"And the flagpole was here," she said, looking across the gorge for those very private silver-birch cabins called Elka Park.

Otto lifted the back of her plaid skirt. "You smell like ferns, like you was ten years old."

Crows could be heard, but not seen.

"Feel good you married me?" (He meant, "Wouldn't you rather have the hotel?")

"Mostly."

"Mostly? What the hell is that?"

"Only don't ask that way," said Rosella in a voice that was harder than she wanted it to be. "Say, 'Do you love me?' and it's nothing but yes."

Otto sulked step-by-step to the car. Rosella opened her hand on gleaned tiny hemlock cones and went after him.

[45]

Liddy drew her thumb along the chromed edge of the sideboard. She decided to smile.

"Mom, I'm going ahead whatever you say, so why don't you say yes and make it nice for both of us."

Rosella couldn't decide anything. She pushed her glasses up and rubbed the sides of her nose. A truck passed, then another.

"This house is too close to the road," she said.

Liddy played exasperation, tsking and rolling her eyes. "Why can't you see what an important opportunity this is for a girl my age? Gosh sake, Mom, do I want to spend my whole life darning socks and pickling beets and all that? Do I?"

Rosella took no offense. She leafed through the paper. A comedy with Joel McCrea was playing.

"Because I'm calling Merle right now and telling her to get the tickets. I mean it."

Rosella thought of how long it had been since Otto had written. Maybe his freighter was in a port he couldn't spell. But she had Prince Valiant, Helen Trent, her chickens and roses to fuss with. Was that why she didn't miss him more?

Liddy dialed six numbers, hung up, and came clattering back.

"You need quieter shoes," her mother said.

"We need you to lend us the money."

Liddy was going to cry.

[67]

There were the same two chickadees that came every day to the feeder.

She said, "Otto, does it hurt bad today?"

He blinked, smiled at the falling snow.

The man on television said, "Tell her what she's won, Johnny."

There was the magazine without pictures which Liddy had sent because it printed her article: "Kings of Song: Armenian Bards in the Seventeenth Century." She picked it up to try to read it again, but the language was thick. Bard? Someplace they had a dictionary, but it meant climbing upstairs. She wondered how Liddy could be a professor of music and not play any instrument.

It was going to be dark early. She noticed surfaces where snow caught: in a line on the back of the iron deer, where the gnome folded his arms and on parts of his cap. John Ostrander drove a sand truck up the road. Probably John. She couldn't see into the cab.

The college was in Oregon, but Liddy called each week, took an interest. Still, the big place in her heart belonged to Carol, with a husband in jail and sloppy kids and running out most nights. She knew this was "wrong," but some things were just there and you didn't decide.

Otto teased her by slurping his tea. He made waggish eyes. The man on television said: "See you next time."

[85]

Girl abusing my arms for the ivy bottles, loud, hair shiny. Married to Jesus and wearing white to show that off, no need so loud and cheerful then try to give pills like the sacrament. Change the rules once you learn following, new tricks for the dog, and marrying Otto in beige, pure as I could be, Mama angry about all the sewing, always true to that, hands on hips, middle of that fire probably, giving hell and hail Columbia. Otto never pretended, fell in love with the way he went under and left before hot afternoon dill cucumber soup and white stoneware bowls in all hands on deck for their day not his to wake up on stage costume faces and white glove pressing—Anita and a black fan three Wolvens Ed and Norma TC who punched him in the railyard confused Connie Fratello who bought the meat market Ethel and Sid the fat Garside kids Shorty and Moira who flew a woman from Kerhonkson with dirty boots and hid inside the hedge me seeing them all. Q

Wind

Not one of them did anything to help.

They didn't plan the menus. They didn't order the food. Or carry the bags in from the car. They didn't tell the couple where they were going—and Howard wasn't a bit better; whether they'd be in or out for dinner, or what the children were doing, either. Even their babysitter, she left the place a mess. As if she'd had that wretched wind in here helping her: the furniture upside down; the children's clothes any which way, scattered all around.

And no one ever thanked her. Not a single word of thanks.

Not for the nice skirt, or the white blouse. Or those nice slacks she'd called about and had sent all the way to town for. Or for the trip itself, all the way down from New York. And look at these new things, not even tried on, just tossed here and there across the room. Did they think a ghost had brought them in here? Didn't they realize it was a person struggling to do something right, to be helpful? And didn't they realize that it couldn't go on like this? That all this mess, that this never having to thank anybody, just couldn't keep on going on?

On this road to town, she didn't know how people could live. The way they'd been built, these roadside condominiums. One up against the other. Without even windows, hardly. And no planting or shrubbery, not even those lousy low cabbage palms. With just the wind blowing in against them, against their flattened, penitentiary roofs.

And over there on the other side of the highway, those ten-story condominiums, with nothing to relieve them, either. No better than those things of the children's, those building blocks that were always getting underfoot, that she was always practically killing herself on.

Yes, it was incredible to her.

The steering wheel—good Lord, it was so windy!—she had to hold tight.

Yes, it was incredible to her that people—that architects, builders, landscapers, and none of them cheap, either—could have made things so ugly.

Yes, that when these architects could have built anything, and when the people living in these things could have chosen to live anywhere, that they could have chosen these.

And that people, when they have a choice, will not choose something beautiful; that people don't care what you give them. No, you could put it right out in front of them, and if you didn't push them into it, they would go on stubbornly refusing what you were offering, what you simply out of the kindness of your heart wanted them to have.

It made her feel tired.

And it especially made her feel tired that here she was driving all the way to town—and in all this wind—just because Audrey Simpson had said, "Why don't you come down and see us all?" Because if Audrey Simpson could be bothered, she could have gotten herself up and come to see them. But those slacks of Ann's, what was going to happen if she wasn't going to drive all the way down to return them? And the blanket covers, that was something she could bet no one had thought of.

So here she was again. Pushed back to this—that if she didn't do it, no one else would.

Well, here was another thing she knew. That driving in this wind was no fun at all, gripping the steering wheel so tight all the time, the car jumping back and forth across the white line —or feeling as if it would, as if it weren't a car at all but something flimsy, something light and aluminum.

As usual at the Bath and Tennis Club here, she was again asking why she had bothered coming. It was ridiculous, she had always thought, the way people came all the way down here just to end up in another city. Because if a city is what they wanted, they should have stayed in New York. And she had always known—hadn't she?—that Audrey didn't care about her at all. No more than Audrey cared for that woman at the check-out counter she was talking to.

And that she didn't care for Audrey, either. That is, that she no longer had time to care for the things Audrey cared for—the counts and duchesses, the continual shopping up and down the same street. If you asked her, hadn't Audrey already bought enough to open a shop, just out of her own closet?

Nor did she care about Audrey's care for herself—never taking more than one macaroon at lunch, always having her massage, no matter what else was about to happen. Or about Audrey's care for the perfect order she ran her staff in—dust to dust, ashes to ashes, was that one kind of order Audrey had never heard of? And about the perfect order of her life with George, which she was so proud about.

"I'll be right back, Virginia, dear. I'm just hopping up to get a little more of that divine arugula," Audrey had said.

And what Audrey would come back with was nothing more than a sprig of it, she could predict.

And look at Audrey up there, in her bathing suit with that long piece of silk cloth—the kind that Ann should be wearing —flapping around her waist in all this wind, and she trying to hold it down at the edge so it kept on looking right.

Yes, indeed, it made her nervous, sitting here with all these people she had known her whole life—Francis Willey complaining about his hounds in Georgia, how in all this wind the hounds couldn't hear their calls, were running haywire. Reevie Rhinelander complaining about her tennis, how the wind made her forget which side of the court she was on; how when she tossed up her ball, it drifted back over her head. Although she couldn't stop herself swinging at it, anyway.

It was funny, she thought to herself as she waited for the car attendant to come around, the way she had gotten so she could barely sit down anymore. "Virginia, can't you sit down?" Francis Willey had said to her. "You're always on the go, you're going to have a heart attack if you keep on going on like this."

Well, the reason she could barely sit down anymore—which no one but Francis Willey had even bothered noticing—was that she was the kind of person who just couldn't stand to see a thing not done. And that they were the kind of people who could just sit there and talk about doing things—probably even in the face of a hurricane—without doing anything. Couldn't any of them see that? That she was just the kind of person who got things done? And that this always taking responsibility is what had made her this nervous?

But she was glad she had remembered about getting the clothes for her baby Elizabeth at that cute little children's store. Because just before she remembered it, she had said something that made her feel sad about herself. She had said, when Reevie Rhinelander asked her, "What brings you down here today, Virginia?" she had said, "Oh, I'm just here today to do a little light shopping."

Even though she had said it in a tone that mocked ever so slightly the phrase "a little light shopping," as if she were picking up a light little one-thousand-dollar dress . . .

Well, she didn't know what it was. Yet in spite of her upbeat tone, it had made her feel sad, it had given her the image of herself driving all by herself down here with just her bag of slacks to return. So that even while they were all still talking, she had thought, I'm so sad, I might as well just drown myself. Which is what she was thinking when she had seen them—those cute adorable little grandchildren of Reevie Rhinelander's—and remembered about the Purple Turtle store, about how cute the clothes were there, and how beautiful her little Elizabeth was—worth all the clothes ever made in this world; and that it was for this—for her darling Elizabeth

—that she was driving all this way, no matter what else in this world might not be right.

And when she was driving home again, past the ten-story condominiums—she pictured miniature people high up in them but protected, and busy with miniature vacuums—past the high Mobil sign, past the signs for the airport, and past the low condominiums—even on a day like today, airless as mausoleums—and finally past the shrubs, miles and miles of them, cactus and cabbage palm; when she was driving past all this, she imagined for some reason that now home felt like home in a way it hadn't when she left it.

She was restless to get home. Restless that nothing happen before she get there. As if the wind that was pushing the cabbage palms down—down almost against the sand—were not the wind at all but a threat like fire that was spreading out in front.

What she imagined was that Ann and John would be there in the big living room, in their tennis whites, and the children in the kitchen that opened off of it, anchored at the table and eating nicely—and the couple not fussing, either. And the way they would rush to her, little John first, headlong, colliding with her at the knees, "Gramma's home, sister," and Elizabeth following in her ladylike manner, as if some force were pushing her from behind, which she was resisting until she had prepared something wry to say, like the last time when she had said, "Grandmother, do you look like a camel, or what?" And, "Do you have something refreshing for me in one of those boxes, or what?"

And she imagined that though the geraniums that hung from the lampposts down Gomez Road were swaying in the wind, and though the casuarinas, which were higher than anything else by far, were bending back in the wind as if they would snap, still she had imagined that here just across the waterway, that here on this secluded island, that here at this house she had built for all of them, even for Howard, it would be windless.

And coming slowly around the corner into her driveway, there was Ann and John's car—so they were home!—and even in the spot she was always asking them to park it in.

But inside, no one was there.

And out the large glass windows, the waterway was choppy.

And no one was watching it; no children were watching it for boats.

Even the pool water, the surface of which she could see when she went up the steps to the plate-glass door, was restless —countless little high-pitched waves being driven against the side of the pool and splashing back to smack into the new ones coming toward them.

She called to say hello. To see if anyone was home.

She went to each of the four bedrooms. Knocking first on Ann and John's door. Then pushing the door open to find no one on the beds. The beds pushed together but made. As if no one had been lying on them, or sitting. Which she had asked them not to do.

So by herself she went back out to the car to get the bags of her shopping and brought them into little Elizabeth's room.

At the Purple Turtle, she had to admit, she had gone a bit crazy.

But if Ann didn't like all the clothes she had spread out on Elizabeth's bed, and over onto the chair, or if they were the wrong size, or not what Elizabeth needed, then Ann could return them. And Ann could get the credit.

But in her opinion, she had done quite well. She had gotten little white shorts, the kind that were so hard to find, that would show a little waist; she had gotten a terry-cloth bathrobe with a little green whale on it, and a bathing suit to match—although she didn't want the child to think about swimming too much, to think that she could swim by herself —and several cute pairs of pink slacks; and a whole lot—maybe too many—of cute T-shirts, the most adorable of which was covered with tiny kites, all blowing this way and that and made of sticks and colored bits of sailcloth, each with its own rib-boned tail. And the shirt itself—the lady in the store had told her—could even become a kite. Although in spite of the lady's explanation—she thought of her little Elizabeth with her thick figure—she didn't see how the shirt became a kite; or how it would do when it had to be cleaned—not tossed into a ma-chine, she didn't suppose.

But she had bought it anyway, she couldn't resist; even if now she could see, it wasn't too practical.

But what she had to do now was make some room on the bed. Because she had, of course, gotten a few nice dresses—she couldn't have the child always looking as if she'd just blown in here on the wind, no one at all caring for her.

Although when she started to lay out the last of the dresses, she felt again that maybe it looked wrong—a child having so much. And that maybe she should keep some for the birthday, or for Christmas, or at least for Easter. Even though when she was carrying them—it was odd—the bags had seemed so light.

So she put all the ones on the chair back into the bag, thinning out those on the bed.

But where were they? It was past five already. And where was Howard? Although she was used to that by now, not know-ing where he was. And it was past time, too, for the couple to be getting the dinner. Why was it that they were all of them always so thoughtless?

Well, maybe they were in the cottage, that was some-thing she hadn't thought of. Something that had taken her by surprise. Its even being there, it was so new.

Not that she thought the children were up there. Because she had been telling them, she had been telling Ann and John over and over that she didn't want the children up there. Since it was so high and since the steps up to it were still without a railing.

Yes, the cottage without its railing, and also the pool, were the two things she was always warning Ann and John about. Warning them that the children had to be watched always, warning them that if there was just the babysitter, the children shouldn't be in the pool. Since there were two of them, and only one of her, the babysitter.

Of course she hadn't been planning to go up the stairs, or even open the door. The thought of it—if they really wanted to know—the thought of that room high up there with only those two beds in it—even if they had been pushed together —was unsteadying. Nowhere, in this wind, that she'd ever want to be.

No, she was just planning to call from below to ask where the children were. Which was, in her opinion, not a lot to ask. And especially since it was past time for dinner—didn't they ever look at a watch now and then?

No, they needn't worry about that—about her going up.

But when she called, "Ann, Ann," she had to call louder. Because her words were hardly audible. As if they couldn't get up from underneath the wind. Or else as if they were blown on top of the wind, forced and jerked along paths above where she was trying to make them go.

So she'd had to go up a few steps higher.

But when she stopped to get her bearings in this wind— she hadn't stopped to listen—she saw the babysitter coming into the driveway in the golf cart with little John, with little John cuddled up close beside her.

And little John had seen her and was waving.

So she'd had to go back down.

And little John was coming toward her, yelling, "Gramma, Gramma!"

But she had to tell him to hush, she had to find out if the

babysitter knew where they all had gone, and why her Elizabeth wasn't with them. And why no one had bothered to leave her a note, or tell her what the plans were.

Well, that babysitter was a perfect moron, not checking that the child was with her parents, and cheeky, too, the way she had said it—Did a babysitter have to be responsible for everything that went on around here?

Nor had she bothered even answering that babysitter, that ridiculous girl who cared only for going out at night.

But she had started right off for the house, and for the pool, not thinking of anything else but the surface of the pool with its many little choppy little waves and worrying just about that: that its surface was all she could picture, nothing deeper.

And saying to herself: Why hadn't she gone out there to check when she first came in? She had known—hadn't she?—that those parents wouldn't, those parents who had left her precious grandchild without anyone to care for her, those parents who had left her precious Elizabeth wandering all alone around the house, not knowing which direction she should turn in—even their child they treated this way, it was unthinkable—just because those parents—if that's what you could call them—had wanted to be alone up there.

Beating so hard is what her heart was doing, from running to get out there, out to that pool; beating so hard it was forcing itself up into her throat until she thought she was going to choke on it.

And at the big glass window, still she could see only the little waves being driven to the edge of the pool, nothing deeper.

And she had had to stop to open it, the big plate-glass door, and ripped her fingernail right off trying to do it, to get it open.

Then she was down the steps—had she seen something dark at the bottom?—and out to the pool.

Yes, but now she could see that it wasn't, thank God, her Elizabeth down there, when she got there finally, but that it was just her two pool chairs, which must have been blown into the deep end, and her large pot of geraniums, and on the surface, up against the filter where she hadn't seen it from the window, a bathing suit of hers.

She stood for a moment. To catch her breath.

She looked for something to sit on.

Then she just leaned back against the wall of the terrace, looking for a moment longer at what had sunk, thank God, beneath all that heavy water, not her Elizabeth.

And at the little waves lapping madly on the surface, so many and so regularly that it seemed it wasn't the wind at all that was causing it, that was causing the water to be stirred up like this without remission, but something mechanical and from underneath.

But the motion was just on the surface. Because the chairs down there were resting absolutely heavy and unbothered. As if their aluminum frames had weighed something now that they had never weighed above water. And resting in the exact position—canted toward each other—as they would be if two people were in them, talking. While her bathing suit—her bathing suit with its disgraceful skirt on it, her bathing suit which at the filter seemed almost moored there, and had not yet sunk—was rippling up and down on the water, rippling in ways that a backbone wouldn't let it, not even a child's backbone, or a dead person's backbone, and the skirt was moving up and down on the waves, too, as it would be if the legs were limp, as it would be if they couldn't do their kicking anymore.

And then the flowerpot. It surprised her how little dirt had come out of it; how little of it had dirtied the pool.

And how permanent it seemed down there where it was.

Which is what she was thinking of—how it seemed too

heavy ever to lift up again—when she heard her little Elizabeth far off saying, "Look what Gramma got me, look what Gramma got me!" And her daughter's voice coming up behind her:

"What's all the fuss about, Mother? Do you always have to be bothering us, Mother? Mother, can't you ever stop disturbing people?" **Q**

The Mountain

The man I met in Gerzett—I think I met him in Gerzett; I can't be quite sure—said something about a fly. It was what he said about the fly that made me remember.

At any rate, I did not notice the man coming toward me because I was reading or sipping a cup of tea or doing both, or perhaps I was simply gazing at the lake. I was looking across the smooth green grass that dipped down toward the lake like a sigh and saw, I think, the silver-blue of the water reflected for a moment in the breast of a bird as it swept down low across my vision.

Naturally, I did not notice the man.

He was not really the sort one notices, even coming toward one, even in those shoes: thick crepe-soled shoes that give beneath the foot with a slight lurch and squeak mournfully as one moves. Besides, I was used to handling this sort of thing, or what I thought was this sort of thing. I went on doing whatever it was I had been doing before.

Even when the fellow was quite close to me, blocking the afternoon light, his shadow before him, I did not look up. It usually works best—ignoring them—I mean, if that is what they are after, which this fellow, in fact, was not. When he began to speak, I did not even hear what he was saying to me, until he had said it twice, and even then it was only the name that I heard. It was the name which struck me; it was not the sort of name one would forget entirely.

All of that month of May I had lingered on somewhat reluctantly in Gerzett. Despite what the doctors had told me about the therapeutic quality of the Swiss air, I found that the place was far too high for me; the air was too thin; I was constantly breathless.

I definitely did not like that lake. Just the thought of that still, trapped water was somehow dreadfully depressing. But it was the mountains, those towering snow-tipped peaks, with their steep craggy treeless surfaces, which filled me with an almost physical malaise, an impression of being shut in, or perhaps it was shut out.

Actually, I've never been able to remain for very long in the mountains. There is something about their stark beauty brooding eternally above one that daunts me and gives me somehow a sense of the impoverishment of life, a sense of doom which can literally bring on an attack of nausea or giddiness in my particular constitution.

Between you and me, I've never really liked Switzerland. The people are courteous, of course, but frightfully dull, and the whole place has always looked somehow "preserved" to me, rather like pickles in a jar. And too many cows, I always say, there are just far too many cows, and as for those wretched cow bells, which wake one in the morning and ring constantly through the day, they are enough to send one dashing off into that lake.

The hotel, which had been recommended to me as secluded and well appointed, turned out, of course, to be somewhat dilapidated. It was quiet, naturally, surrounded as it was by acres of lawns and wooded areas and that depressing lake. There were the usual sort of mixed borders and spreading oaks and sad cypresses. But the whole place was not a little in need of repair. It had seen better days.

Actually, it rather amazed me that the place had any clients at all. It was one of those hotels so refined in its elegance that the elegance was really only visible in the price of the room. The bathrooms, though fortunately very clean, had undoubtedly not been touched since 1930, and the walls of the corridors and dining room had been painted some sort of ghastly pale lime-green that seemed to glow with an almost ghostly light.

At that time of year, there was hardly anyone there except a handful of solid English dowagers whom I heard at mealtimes rather than saw, bent over their plates, beside the potted palms, scraping their way noisily through the indigestible food in the vast half-empty dining room.

But, I must say, I had managed to secure a not entirely uncomfortable room after a long and vituperative argument with the hotel manager. I insisted on that particular accommodation because it was away from the main body of the hotel, almost entirely self-contained and consequently very quiet— I suffer from insomnia and absolutely anything wakes me—and because of the honeysuckle which grew up the wall and almost into my window.

The gardener had had to come and cut back the creeper from the window while I was staying in that room. He had come and hacked at the plants with a blunt instrument, a short semicircular blade or sickle, and I had had to ask him not to cut the creepers back too much but to let them grow along the windowsill so that I could see them from my bed when I woke in the mornings.

The room was large and sunny, with a wide soft double bed and a reading lamp which you could actually read by, a rarity in hotels, I always find; a steel table and chair on a not unbearably narrow private area where I was able to enjoy the weather, which was, I will admit, passably fair for that time of year: the light clear and bright from dawn to sunset and the wind still.

And the doctors, after all, had gone on at considerable length to recommend the place to me, praising the dry, clean air and the sunny climate, what they had the audacity to call the plain healthy food, and pointing out that the secluded nature and general restfulness of the place were ideal for someone suffering from my eternal complaint; so I stayed on for a while, partly out of lethargy—the spring has always made me, not restless, but apathetic—but also waiting to see if the doctors' advice might eventually prove to be salutary.

Every evening, from five to seven, I sat on the main terrace of the hotel overlooking the lake under the wooden window boxes of multicolored geraniums. I had arranged my time carefully; it is my custom to arrange my time carefully and to follow my schedule exactly: I broke each day up into a number of identical segments which, by their abiding uniformity, never gave me the impression that the day was passing either too fast or too slowly: every morning I took as lengthy a walk as I could manage in the woods, lunched generally in some restaurant in the town, and came back to the hotel for a long siesta in my room with the shutters closed; after a bath, I spent the rest of the afternoon on the terrace looking over the lake, with a cup of tea or a drink, my inhalator in my lap in its zippered bag, a book or the newspaper or sometimes nothing at all, just the changing light in the leaves to amuse me.

Of course, at night, at times, there were men—not the type who could cause one any trouble.

As for this one, the one who came over to me on the terrace of the hotel, he said, I believe, after some preliminary excuses for the disturbance he was causing, "Were you not related to Claire Richdale?" or perhaps, "You were a friend of Claire Richdale's, it seems to me?" or something of that sort.

I do not pretend to reproduce the man's particular vernacular. I'm afraid I did not pay sufficient attention to his words to render them with any sort of authenticity but can only attempt to give the general gist of what he said. He spoke, I believe, without any sort of elegance, but at the same time as a man of not a little education would speak and, as far as I noticed, with a slight accent which was familiar to me and immediately marked the man as coming from the place I had left a considerable time ago.

I do remember the name the man said and the way he said that name, which was what made me look up for a moment at the man who was standing before me. There was something about the way he said the name, something almost tentative and tremulous, which took me by surprise; it did not seem to match the rest of the man.

Even then I glanced at him for only a second and went on

doing whatever it was I had been doing before: just gazing or reading my book or sipping tea. The name, though I recognized it vaguely, meant nothing to me, and the man actually interested me even less, of course.

I do not have a clear recollection of the man's face. All I remember was that there was something vaguely dark about his presence: either it was the hair or the eyebrows, or even the eyes or the skin, or perhaps even the fact that the fellow was not particularly well shaven; whatever it was, there was some impression of darkness to the man, that's all I can say, never having bothered, then or later, to peruse his countenance with much interest. He had on a white, not absolutely clean shirt, open at the neck, with no tie but the hint of some sort of vulgar gold chain around the neck, and beneath that what I imagined might be one of those hirsute chests; a shiny jacket, rather too broad at the shoulders and too narrow at the waist for my liking; a pair of dark tight trousers which might have been navy or black or even dark green, which showed far more than I wished to see of the man's masculinity; and those shoes which squeaked, went on squeaking, as he shifted his weight.

But even then the chap did not remove himself but continued to hover there beside me, blocking my afternoon light and view of the lawns and the trees.

To get the man's shadow out of my way, or because I could not really do otherwise and remain within the bounds of common courtesy, or finally, because of the name, or the way the man said the name, I motioned him to the chair opposite. It was all the invitation the fellow required. He sat down with his back to the lake. As he sat down, something about the way he seated himself, or perhaps it was more something not a little familiar about the way he held his head or leaned forward across the table, I can't quite pinpoint what it was about the chap as, naturally, I was not really paying him any sort of attention at all, but still, something did give me the impression that this was not the first time I had seen the man on the terrace; the fellow might have been there before; I might have seen him before.

As far as I remember, the chap launched into the conversation by asking me if I knew what had happened to the woman whose name he had already mentioned.

"What happened to whom?" I suppose I must have asked him, and gone on watching the boats coming back to the land, after a day on the water, with their sails folded around their booms.

At times I liked to watch the way the boats slid through the water at the end of the day, coming silently into the shelter of the harbor. There was something slow and peaceful about the way the hull of the boat cut cleanly through the calm surface of the water which satisfied me and distracted me from the presence of those mountains, which I felt hung over the place so somberly, like some sort of warning of disaster.

By that time of evening the water was a steel-blue; the mountains were already dark. They loomed above us, I felt.

I suppose I must have been talking about the boats while the fellow was going on about this woman, whom he called Claire Richdale—one of those conversations one engages in so frequently, you know what I mean, the kind which runs along parallel lines.

I made a vague attempt to fit the name to a face, but I didn't exert myself overmuch. I was still under the impression the man was using some trumped-up and rather unimaginative excuse to come over to my table and strike up some sort of conversation with me, which I presumed he would relinquish —the conversation, that is—without much persuasion, to take up other, more promising prospects. I suppose I attempted to keep the conversation, as the fellow seemed to feel obliged to converse, as anodyne as possible. I think I said, "We've been lucky this month with the weather, haven't we?" or some such remark about the weather, thinking the fellow would be glad to follow my lead.

The pink rambling roses which grew along the wall of the terrace had already been covered over to protect them from the cold of the night. I remember wondering whether this protection was absolutely necessary and why it was the hotel gardener felt these roses needed this particular type of covering during the night.

However, the fellow did nothing to improve his position by going on to apologize at length and, as far as I can recollect, in the most unoriginal tiring way, for this intrusion. He kept insisting that he had no desire to disturb me, that he was not accustomed to disturbing solitary women, particularly attractive women, or perhaps he said elegant women, something of that sort, that he was aware it was really quite rash of him, etc., etc., none of which I believed for a moment, naturally, and all of which did more than a little to add to my growing annoyance. He continued to maintain, with exasperating insistence, despite the fact that I gave him no encouragement whatsoever, that he was quite certain he had seen me with this woman, or that I was related in some way to this woman, or had even been close friends with this woman he called Claire Richdale. Not only did the chap's words annoy me, but for a reason which was not yet apparent, they began to make me not a little uneasy, although I scarcely knew with what.

However, I let him run on for a while, rather as one does a horse which has bolted, you know, hoping he would eventually tire and come to a stop of his own volition.

I have often found this an excellent means of coping with bores, and how many people are there who are not bores? The world, of course, is peopled mainly with bores, isn't it? I find it not unpleasant, though, to just sit back and relax, awash in a murmur of half-heard words, letting them ebb and flow like waves around me, my attention wandering where it will, while the other, the speaker, goes on, sails forth quite contentedly onward; it is quite amazing how long people will go on quite contentedly without requiring any sort of encouragement. One can generally pick up the thread at some crucial point, or simply add a nod or a grunt here or there, and no one is the wiser. I have always asked myself how people can possibly believe anyone would want to listen to all of that.

So I sat there, as I often do, hardly listening, or only listening sufficiently to follow the gist of what the fellow was saying—going on with my tea, I believe, or perhaps I had already moved from tea to a gin-and-tonic with lime, and only conscious, really, to tell you the truth, of the fact that the light was fading rapidly, the sun was sinking, the mountains were black above us, and that the fellow had somehow shifted his weight as he talked so that he was leaning rather uncomfortably close to me, breathing almost directly into my face.

It was not, I realized afterward, only his closeness that made me uncomfortable.

"Hardly that," I said finally, in reference to this supposed close friendship or relation that he was so certain had linked me to this woman called Claire. I unzipped my inhalator, pumped a couple of times, and repeated, "It could hardly have been that," in a somewhat exasperated tone at that point, wishing then to rid myself of this importunate fellow. "That could only be a gross overstatement," I said, and began, I must say, at that point, to wonder vaguely why the man kept on going on about this business, whatever it was, and how I was going to get rid of him. I didn't imagine that a man of this sort had anything of interest to tell me about anyone, and least of all about this woman, whoever she was.

I said, "Actually, I don't think I could really say I was close friends with anyone, for that matter."

As far as I remember, that remark silenced him for a while, but still he did not move. We went on sitting there, on the terrace, under the geraniums—I've never particularly liked geraniums: too bright, too stiff, the sort of flowers one finds in the window boxes of Swiss banks—the fellow leaning half across the table with his shiny sleeve brushing my arm.

But even then the chap did not give up. After a pause, he renewed his attack. He asked me to try to consider where I might have met this woman, if I might not have been at school with this woman, or have met her, perhaps, at some party, even as a child. Would I not, he begged me, with an urgency in his voice which struck me then as nothing but tiresome, because I was beginning to realize that the fellow was going to be not a little difficult to ignore, was not going to simply get up and dissolve into the darkening sky, nor was he going to settle, even, for what it was that I had originally thought he was after, which after all would have been something I could have handled, could have understood, which I could have taken or left as I wished—would I not, he asked me, reflect carefully and make absolutely certain that I had not even been at school with this woman. Could boarding school have been the place where we had met?

In an attempt to sum up, to conclude the matter in some way that might be satisfactory to this man and thus shake the fellow off, I did, perhaps, make some sort of an effort to place the name. I said, "Perhaps we were at school together. Maybe that's it. I suppose we might have been. The name is vaguely familiar. We might even have been in the same class at some point. I rather think we were. Perhaps she failed down into my class or they put me up into hers. I really don't remember. It was a long time ago," and pulled my shawl—the black wool one with the red flowers embroidered around the edge—around my shoulders and snapped the flap of my handbag in preparation for a move. I added, still hoping to change the subject and thus rid myself of the fellow or at least this tiresome conversation, "The light is fading fast. Odd how it lingers and then suddenly gets dark, isn't it?" or something of that sort.

But the man refused to be put off. He still wanted to know if I knew what had happened to this woman, as though it were possible that, not even remembering who she was, I could possibly have known or wanted to know what had happened to her.

"No idea. Whoever she is, I certainly haven't seen the woman for years," I said.

But even that reasonable statement did not satisfy the chap. He could not believe I had not read something about the matter in the papers somewhere or had not spoken to someone who would have told me what had happened to the woman.

I tried, summarily, to explain that I had left all of that far behind me, that my life out there might almost have belonged to someone else. I believe I said something like: "I haven't been back there for years. I move around a lot, you know. Never stay anywhere for very long. Quite lost touch with all of that. Always found that place killingly boring, myself. I prefer Europe these days. I have a place in the Cotswolds where I keep my things. This is rather a pretty spot, don't you think?"

It seems to me that it was at that point in the conversation —but I may, of course, not be remembering all of this in the order in which it actually happened, particularly as I was hardly listening to the chap, was paying much more attention to the water and the mountains and even the geraniums than to what the man was trying to say to me—that the fellow said he was sure he had seen me with this woman he called Claire Richdale at her house. He said something about my having spent a day with the woman at her house. I remember this clearly, as the chap repeated this supposition more than a couple of times. The fellow, as I remember, was the sort who repeated himself continuously, whether it was because the topic excited him particularly or because this was his habit, I did not know, but I did know that his propensity to repetition added not a little to the general dreariness of his conversation.

The man said something to the effect that he thought I might have visited at this Claire's home, spent a day with the woman, and that he might have seen me there at that particular moment. I suppose I answered something along the lines of: "It is possible I visited her home once. I was often invited to the homes of my school friends and sometimes I went. I might have visited these people you are talking about. I do have a vague recollection of some dreary house, now that you mention it, and even some relatives who might have been hers: a mother, perhaps, or an aunt, perhaps more than one aunt, something like that. So I suppose it's possible you saw me there."

Then I made another, last-ditch effort to shut the fellow up—I was deadly bored by that point, reduced to plucking off the petals from a geranium and crushing the stem between finger and thumb to keep myself occupied—you can imagine. I attempted to get rid of the chap entirely by assuring him that, despite all my efforts, I could honestly not remember another thing about this woman. I believe I told him, what was certainly the case, that I really didn't have a very good memory for that sort of thing. I said, "Curiously, I tend to remember things more than people. Anyway, one always remembers the most insignificant, the most useless of details, and forgets the essentials, don't you think?"

This remark, however apt, and surely it was, in this case, particularly apt, seemed to have little or no effect on the man. I remember how he sat there: by then the man's face was so close to me I could hear the sound of his breathing. He breathed audibly, with his lips open on the dark of his mouth. I was left no recourse but my inhalator, which I pulled out once again and pumped.

I said, still trying to be courteous—I believe good manners are probably the most useful of all the virtues—but by then almost ready to get up and leave the fellow sitting there in his shiny jacket and his squeaking shoes: "You know, it really is getting rather late. I remember so little about this woman. I am honestly trying to tell you everything I know, but I don't think I can help you at all. I may have spent a day with her, it's quite possible, I do remember something about that house.

She may have asked me to come and spend the day with her and she may even have talked to me, told me the story of her life, told me . . . heaven knows what she might have told me. But I really have no recollection of what she said or what I might have said or what I might have done. It was a long time ago, and besides, none of us listens much to one another, do we? In my experience people just don't listen. They may even ask questions, but they don't listen to the answers."

But even this had apparently little effect. The man's tenacity was beyond my comprehension. I could in no way grasp what it was the chap was after, with his incessant questions and his continuous flow of words. Of course, I had no idea, nor did I particularly care what the man was after with me, I had only one thought at that point, which was, as it is with a fly which buzzes against one's face in the night, to get rid of the fellow.

Unbelievably, the chap went on talking, though I can hardly tell you what it was he said to me at that point. I believe there was some question of a name. The fellow seemed not a little anxious to know if this Claire had mentioned the name of someone, perhaps some man she might have been involved with or something of that sort. All of this was interspersed in a most confused and irrational way with various odd bits of information about the man himself; I believe he actually tried to tell me something about his own life, his mother, his father, a house he had once rented, a straw mattress, his profession or his lack of a profession, what he was doing up there in the mountains, but naturally, I paid no attention at all to any of that at the time.

As far as the name was concerned—the name the man thought this woman might have mentioned to me—I told the man I had never been very good with names. I said, "My goodness, I even have difficulty introducing my own mother."

Finally, I told the fellow that it was the time that, in the normal course of things, I went in for dinner, that I found it wiser not to eat too late and that the hors d'oeuvres were much better before anyone else attacked them. On Sunday nights the hotel always served a buffet dinner and I presume this must have been a Sunday evening.

At that point I almost forgot the chap, who had slumped again into silence, sitting in the rapidly fading light. I was thinking about the amazing quantities of food people took from buffet tables; the way they piled up their plates and how they managed to eat all of that and remain so thin. Perhaps I told the chap that personally I found the whole business of eating rather a bore. I could never decide what to eat, particularly in that place where the choice was generally between a *bifteck aux pommes frites* and a *bifteck aux pommes frites.*

He said suddenly—I suppose he may have been staring at me or what he could see of me in that dim light—I remember this clearly: "You know, you look like her. You really do. There's definitely something about you that makes me think of her. There's some resemblance."

I had lost the thread of his conversation to the point that I replied, "I look like whom?" When he had made it evident that he was still talking about the same woman, I suppose I replied that I couldn't imagine why he thought I looked like this Claire Richdale, though to tell you the truth, I had great difficulty conjuring up her features at all. The only impression I had of the woman's face was that it was quite probably a most ordinary one, a face, as far as I could remember, without any sort of distinction at all.

To which I believe he replied, "You have the same fair skin which burns easily."

I said abruptly, with the desire that this would close our discussion, "It starts to get cool at around this hour. It is really rather chilly this evening, don't you find? It is definitely time for me to go into dinner. Please excuse me now."

But the fellow's expansive presence did not undergo any sort of contraction. He could not let me go. He only crushed the book of matches he held in his hand and went on sitting there; I was beginning to feel the chap was as immovable as the mountains above us. He begged for just a minute more of my time. He was still certain that I might be able to remember something. He seemed quite unable to let the matter lie and to get up and leave me to go in for my dinner.

After that I hardly listened to what the man said. I heard but barely registered what the man was saying. At the time I was only aware that he became most insistent, and that a flood of words came from him. Afterward, I was able to recollect some of what the man said to me, but at the time, I paid little attention to his words. Afterward, I was to remember more than I wanted to remember of the man's words, but that was later.

Finally, as I was about to simply get up while the man was rambling on in this almost incoherent way about the night he had spent with this woman and how young and foolish he had been at the time, about the importance of my recollecting or the importance of his knowing or even the importance to the general public of my remembering whatever it was he was begging me to remember: what this woman had said, or some name this woman might have said, or something of that sort, the fellow put his hand on my arm, I suspect in his eagerness to retain me, as he told me, what I actually knew by then, anyway, that someone must have done away with this woman in mysterious circumstances.

It was not possible for me to get up at that point; all I could do was to pull my shawl about my shoulders and cross my arms and watch the rambling roses along the wall, lit by the light from the dining room within, under the netting which covered them over against the cold of the night. I was obliged to sit there for a moment at least; it would hardly have been appropriate to leave right then.

I sat for a while in silence staring at the flowers and then, my eyes drawn upward despite myself, staring at the mountains, whose darkness had almost completely merged with the dark of the night. Though even the outlines of the mountains had gone, could only be imagined, felt, the night was full of their ominous form. I sensed their presence huddled over us;

the sense of foreboding they inspired conglomerated, gathered force in their physical absence.

I was suddenly quite overcome with hunger and tiredness, worn out suddenly by this man's insistence, the boredom his presence provoked, or simply by the length of time I had been sitting in the same place. I had been exposed for too long. The night had grown cool, the mist had risen from the lake, and for a moment I shivered. I was afraid I might have caught cold sitting out in the damp evening air.

At that point, too, something else happened, which I think I should mention: I realized that the man had moved, had somehow taken my wrist, had his hand on my wrist, was holding, gripping, not my hand, but my wrist. His face, as far as I could see in the dim light, was quite red and he appeared to me to be sweating slightly, beads of sweat clung to his forehead, and his dark hair was not a little damp around the hairline.

I let my arm lie in his hand. I looked down at the man's hand. He had long, fine, blunt-tipped fingers; deft hands; strong, agile hands; hands that were very clean, the nails carefully manicured; he wore a diamond ring set in gold on the little finger. The ring looked too small for him. His hands, like the way he said the woman's, Claire Richdale's, name, surprised me; they didn't seem to fit the man.

It crossed my mind then that one might sleep with this man or not sleep with this man and that it would come to exactly the same thing.

I rose then and left the man sitting there.

The dining room seemed particularly lugubrious to me that evening. It was a large room which led off one of the lounges and looked over the lake. At that hour, though, the heavy green-velvet curtains were drawn across the windows and billowed gently in the evening breeze. The whole room, for some reason, I thought that evening, resembled some underwater region.

The lime-green walls seemed to me to cast a sickly glow, accentuated by the discreet lighting of the small shaded table lamps, so that even the white tablecloths and the limp pink carnations in their silver vases, reflecting the green, glowed, seemingly phosphorescent. The potted palms in the corners of the room, I observed, appeared to fold and unfold the fingers of their leaves in the slight breeze, like sea anemones.

There was no one in the room except a few guests who sat wrapped in the anonymity of their age and wealth, huddled over their soup. There was almost no sound in the room, as though, I imagined, the pervading gloom had silenced the guests. Besides the waiter's discreet murmuring and the scrape of silver on porcelain, there was nothing to be heard.

I sat at my table wondering why on earth the walls had been painted such a ghastly green. I am not a little sensitive to colors, and the green jarred on my nerves particularly that evening. The duck which I had ordered was definitely a mistake, and even the bottle of wine I had chosen, a not inexpensive bottle of Dole, was not enough to muffle my mood.

My encounter with the importunate man on the terrace and the fate of the barely remembered woman he had spoken of had almost entirely slipped my mind, I was certainly not thinking of either of them, but something about the man's words must have unsettled me. The stillness of the room, which generally went by unnoticed, or was welcomed, troubled my nerves.

I looked around at the room, suddenly struck by the absurdity of it all: the silver shining, the ridiculous tubular flower bowls on each table, the half-dead, drooping carnations, each object in its well-chosen place, all the apparent solidity of a supposedly well-organized world. For a moment the whole room seemed to shift slightly, to tremble, and an absurd thought crossed my mind: I thought I heard the sound of the fellow's crepe-soled shoes on the parquet floor.

I was even drawn, for some unaccountable reason, to exchange a few pleasantries with my neighbor in the lounge after the meal over a cup of coffee, something I had naturally never done before, a ridiculous elderly woman whom I had always avoided, who dined alone and wore the same absurd black taffeta hat every night to dinner and generally tucked a couple of oranges into her knitting bag before retiring.

In my room I lay on my bed and actually smoked a cigarette. I gave it up—cigarette smoking, that is—years ago, naturally, with my complaint, but I always keep a pack of filter-tipped Dunhills handy for emergencies such as this one.

I lay there with only the bedside lamp lit, inhaling, drawing the smoke deep into my lungs, savoring the nicotine and the thought of what it was doing to my lungs, voluptuously—it was, of course, strictly against doctor's orders—I even washed the cigarette down with a stiff neat whiskey. A bottle of that, too, I keep in my room for medicinal purposes. I remember thinking that I had no wish, anyway, to live on for as long as these same doctors would have liked me to go on living and to go on paying their bills.

I stubbed out my half-finished cigarette and tried to read, but with little success. I was unable to concentrate. What I was thinking of as I lay there was the dormitory at school, the light in the dormitory at school.

I could see then that, in the dormitory, the light was silver. The moon lit the room. The mosquito nets, which hung from the row of narrow beds, were drawn back, gathered into thick coils at the head of the beds.

There was a smell of oranges, someone had smuggled an orange into the room from dinner and the orange, or rather the skin of the orange, perfumed the air. It was very hot, although the windows were wide open.

I do not know what season it was. The seasons out there are hardly seasons, they change fast, with no twilight pauses: no melancholy autumnal moments or gauzy spring promises; summer slips into winter almost imperceptibly. It is always more or less hot and more or less humid.

The girls stood on the beds and threw a pillow from bed to bed, giggling, bouncing, waving their arms wildly, their hair flying, bending over to clutch their hollow stomachs in silent laughter, whispering in loud hoarse whispers. The penalty for dropping the pillow was the removal of an article of clothing. That was the rule of the game.

The girl was wearing little clothing at the start of the game. She jumped up and down on the bed, her half-formed breasts naked, her puerile body tight in her moist skin and silver in the light of the moon. I threw the pillow high and hard, so that she reached for it, her arms flailing the air; she fumbled; she teetered, and almost fell.

It was somewhere around ten o'clock, I think, when the telephone rang. I was not really surprised, I suppose, to hear the man's voice.

As I remember it, he began once again by apologizing, but I cut him short this time and simply asked him what he wanted. There was a pause.

Finally the chap asked if he might see me again.

I hesitated a moment, considering. I stood with the receiver in my hand, staring at the bowl of red roses on the dressing table: twelve red roses sent by an admirer; their heads drooped and a fine coating of slime lined their stems. I'm not quite sure why I then said what I did, but it may have had something to do with the flowers.

I told the man I had met on the terrace that if he wanted to see me to obtain information about the woman he had been talking about all that afternoon, there was no point in his coming.

He then made his intentions sufficiently clear.

To be absolutely certain there would be no mistake, I told him he might come to my room then, but that I would not expect him to stay long. I told him I always went to sleep early, which was not actually a lie—I often do go to bed early with a book, not even answering my phone after a certain hour. In this way, I thought, I would avoid any other lengthy conversations. As it turned out, I did avoid any lengthy conversations —the man said hardly more than a dozen sentences—but I was not prepared for what I actually got.

By the time the man arrived in my room I had bathed, perfumed, and powdered my body and was already partly undressed. This was not particularly for the man's benefit but simply a ritual I always performed before any such encounter. Such rituals I find are what enable one to get through life, though there are times when they seem almost too much effort. I had perfunctorily brushed out my hair and let it lie loose around my shoulders—not out of any sort of coquetry, but so that the hairpins I use for my chignon would not dig into the back of my neck. I was already feeling worn out with the effort of all this activity and beginning, as is so often the case, to regret ever having told the man to come to my room, when he rang my doorbell.

I cursorily inspected myself in the full-length mirror in the bathroom. I was attired, I believe, in nothing much more than my short pink silk shift—not the black one—and my black sandals.

As an adolescent I always felt I was too tall and too thin —all arms and legs and eyes. My stepfather, a military man, who finally received his just deserts, kicked in the head by a horse—though there were moments when I thought that even this end was too quick and painless for the man and that I might have enjoyed seeing him lie and suffer for a while— spent his time telling me, among other things of this sort, that I was too tall and that, above all, my feet were too large.

However, the advantage of such a figure—I'm talking

about my figure, of course—is that with the years—I'm not, of course, going to commit the indiscretion of telling you my age, but leave you to come to some reasonable conclusion on your own—there is not much flesh to sag or fall. I think I can say, without much vanity, that I have retained a deceptively youthful appearance, in certain kind lights—I always say, past a certain age, women should come out only at night. At any rate, what I saw in the mirror that night, while the man was knocking on my door—I let him cool his heels out there for a while—did not entirely displease me.

I noticed, too, with some relief, that the man, when I finally opened the door to him and he stepped into my room, had changed his shirt to a clean one of some rather more attractive transparent material and he smelled of some not unpleasant eau de cologne. He was, however, wearing the same shoes, though I noticed he must have given, or had them given, a polish, but that they continued to squeak as mournfully as ever as I led him across to the bed.

The maid had removed the bedcover, and I had lit the bedside lamp—I like to see whom I'm making love to, naturally. I let the man commence with the proceedings without any further preliminaries.

It was as we were both sprawled across my bed, and were already somewhat in disarray, that the man spoke of the fly. The fellow, as I remember, was reclining beside me, or rather against me, hardly even as clothed as I was. I believe he had on nothing more than the gold chain which he wore around his neck and which dangled back and forth in the hair on his chest. He had risen up on one elbow, so as to look down at me, or rather to watch both his hand, I suppose, and my body, while all the while touching my body.

He was not unschooled in the art. I allowed him to work his way freely from my upper extremities to the lower, which he accomplished with not a little ease, his hand maneuvering craftily with the straps of my shift so as to expose as much flesh as he could, going on deftly with some method and some skill, lingering in the appropriate places, doing nothing in too hurried a fashion, nor did he stall for too long, his touch sufficiently strong without being rough—I remember thinking that the fellow would have known how to shampoo hair excellently, that his touch would have been just the thing for a really good shampoo, that it was a pity that I couldn't think of some way to have him give me a shampoo; as he touched me, I let him press his own swollen member against me or, rather, against the remaining thin silk of my shift, which was all that still divided us and which I had allowed him to work down and up, to cover nothing much more than my waist and buttocks.

I lay there with my hands folded under my head and my gaze on the ceiling—there was quite a pretty molding on the ceiling of that room—letting him touch me—his caresses were not unpleasant, after all—but with not a little disinterest, letting him go through the motions; I was certainly in no way excited by his hands or his body—there was nothing exciting about the fellow, I felt.

There was nothing actually wrong with the body, which was tanned for that time of year, broad-chested and slim-hipped, and the legs were really not bad at all, but rather too short it seemed to me—he was probably an inch or so shorter than I am—and I've never been one, though I know there are some who do, to go for that much dark hair on the chest.

At this point in the lovemaking, if you could call it that, when I was beginning to wonder whether it would be worth my while to go through with the whole business or if it would not be wiser to end the proceedings with some trumped-up excuse —a sudden stomach cramp or nausea, or even a qualm of conscience, a husband I had not mentioned, perhaps, who could be dragged in at the last minute to get me out of the final act—without any apparent reason, and without slowing down in any way the movement of his hand or stopping stroking, whatever it was he was stroking at that moment, the fellow made that remark about the fly. I think what he said was: "But she would never have hurt a fly." I'm not absolutely certain of his words, but what I do know is what happened as he said those words.

I remembered something about the woman he was talking about, the woman he called Claire Richdale. A vivid image of this woman came to me.

The woman was in a large sunlit room with two or perhaps three beds. I saw her, this Claire Richdale, from behind, bending down, squatting on her haunches at first and then actually getting down onto her hands and knees and scooping at a small spider, a button spider, I believe they are called—a tiny black spider—pushing a stiff piece of white paper against the carpet, chasing the spider with a piece of white paper, chasing it along the edge of the mauve carpet onto the parquet floor, again and again, turning the paper as it ran one way and then the other, until she caught it on the edge of the page and ran to the window to set the creature free.

She threw open the window with one arm and the spider out into the creeper with the other, and then she turned to face me. The bay window which gave onto the garden was open and the wind whipped the loose sleeves of the woman's dress against her arms. I saw her sleeves flapping against her arms in the wind from the open window. That was what I saw more clearly than anything else in that initial image which came to me: the wide, loose sleeves of her dress; that was what I noticed more than anything else and certainly I noticed that more than her face or even her body, though I cannot tell you exactly of what material the sleeve was made: something soft like shantung or crepe de chine or silk of some sort, something almost transparent flapping, beating against her arms.

While I let the man go on touching my body, his hands descending into the inner recesses of my body, I was thinking of this woman he called Claire Richdale standing in the early-morning sunlight with the bay window open behind her. I could see her quite clearly, almost as though magnified by memory: her arms and the sleeves of her dress flapping gently against her skin; I could see the blond hair on her plump rounded arms and the pale freckles on her honey-colored skin. For some reason the image was exciting to me.

And I was enjoying the man.

It was only when the man had gone that it occurred to me that he had never mentioned his name. All that evening he had been saying the name of this Claire Richdale, but he had never mentioned his own name.

When the man had gone, I rose from the rumpled bed and walked around tidying up the room: remaking the bed carefully, emptying the ashtray and putting the glass away, actually wiping the trace of his shoes from the parquet floor—I cannot abide any sort of disorder—and touching my things: my books: the Austen, the Henry James, the Naipaul, and the Virginia Woolf; the silver brush-and-comb set; the photo of Mother, as a young woman, in its silver frame; the cut-glass bowl; the petit-point cushion; my rings; the cameo brooch; the creams for my face; the clothes in my closet; my suitcases and the straw bag I used on my walks. Somehow the room looked bare to me, as though something was missing. It even occurred to me that the man might have taken something from me, but when I checked, nothing was actually gone.

I took a long shower and scrubbed my skin with a loofah, dusted and perfumed my body, creamed my face. I felt a sudden need for air. I went over and opened the window and stood there gasping for a while, taking in great deep gulps of night air. I realized, as I stood there, that a light rain was falling. I could hear the sound of the water dripping into the gutters and smell the damp earth. The weather had changed.

I stood looking up at what I knew were the mountains, trying to make out their shape in the mist and the dark of the night. There was no moon visible over Gerzett, not even a lone star in the sky. The heavy presence of the mountains, unseen, was suddenly quite unbearable to me. I felt an attack of my complaint coming on; a sudden breathlessness overwhelmed me; I reached for my inhalator. I shivered and began to cough. I was certain I was feverish. I had caught cold. I had been rash remaining so long on the terrace that evening talking to a stranger, and then standing before the window in the damp night air after a hot shower. I knew all too well how dangerous a cold could be for someone with my illness. I wrapped myself hurriedly in a gown and climbed into bed, but I was unable to sleep. As I lay there tossing back and forth, alternately hot and then cold, through what remained of the night, that absurd thought came to me again.

It seemed to me that I could still hear, would go on hearing, in the rustlings and heavings, in the creaks and the muffled cries, in all the anonymous sounds of the night, the man's crepe-soled shoes squeaking. **Q**

The Deer

[I]

As a boy in the barber's chair,
the razor raising the fine hairs
along my neck, the large stuffed moose
and deer heads mounted on the wall
seemed alive, calm, waiting. Their big,
intelligent eyes followed me
whichever chair I got. Sometimes
I would imagine their bodies
continuing behind the walls,
into the shop next door, and that
in one quick move they might withdraw
their heads from the plaques, or push through,
cracking the mirrors and causing
even the barbers to cry out.

[II]

Another five minutes and I
might have come face to face with him,
the buck that broke through Jim Friday's
barber-shop window. But that day
I rushed home from work on foot, by
a route vastly more familiar
than the one he must have taken
in from the woods, the miles he'd come.
So that had I slowed down, I might
have come upon that scene, before
the buck backed out of the smashed shop,
hit a car, and the cops showed up
to pump him, I read, full of shot.
You can't talk down a beast like that . . .

[III]

I might have come to that window,
or what was once a window, where
the ten-point, two-hundred-pound buck
stood in the still-showering glass,
bleeding—and seen Jim, his scissors
and comb suspended, and the boy
in the chair, wisps of hair falling
still. And I think I would have looked
across that trophy filling up
the tiny shop with its two chairs,
at the small boy who was living
my childhood dream or nightmare.
But the boy would be looking past
the deer, past me, out the window
blown to bits, where the suddenly
limitless world was pouring through.

Country Airport

From the two-lane all we can see
past the tall corn is an old shack,
antenna-less, vined, windows dark,
and a wind sock on a pole, slack,

and from here easily a flag.
But no sign of a runway—just
a gouged access road to the shack,
with a tethered horse, raising dust

with its pendulum tail. Some homes
up the way interrupt the view,
but there's no one and, oddly, no
craft in sight at this rendezvous

for small planes. It must be abandoned,
our map and the cashier in town
must be wrong. Dust marbles the horse.
We could see him standing unbound

as the corn finds the tarmac cracks,
and covers the asphalt, until
the landing strip disappears,
and the wind sock is one more tall

plant, a tassel on a stalk. Back
to their homes, back from the wide fields
their fathers must have plowed (seen from
school windows), in from guessing yields,

the farmers who let this runway
run down, left the tarmac untarred,

so with its one room and worn flag
it resembles an old schoolyard,

are just now coming into view,
their tractors small as bumblebees
on the horizon, while children
come to back screens and watch through trees.

for Bill Fielding

Once by the Lake

We were sitting in the gnarled fingers
of pine roots, the lake lapping before our boots,
at our feet a small fire of twigs and stones
and in our hands a small fire passed between us.
Lightly the sweet corn-on-the-cob smell
puffed from the pipe, and puffed from our mouths
in the cold air. The stars were massed above us,
and down the lake the hills in the reclining
human shape we would assume before we knew.
And on the other side of the lake, in camp,
the children were turning into their dreams.
As we stared out across the blackness,
I think already we were looking into
the future, and must have known even then,
although we'd say otherwise, that we'd never
return there, together, unless by
returning we meant to forget why we'd come
again, as there, that night, we would not
have wanted to put to words what had brought us
to the lake at all, but just to sit and watch
the breath leaving our mouths and meeting the
      smoke
from our little fire, knowing that returning
could never be as right as that night in which
we found ourselves, with roots, lake, hills, and
      stars.

Waiting for a Letter

The one-armed bandit
called the mailbox
has robbed me again.
I caught it this morning,
red-handed.

Going on with you
is like leaving novels
unfinished—the characters
always at revealing,
pivotal points of action.

Here the trees
unburden themselves
of that they held most near.

If there is a season
for cutting connections,
this is it—

the leaves
changing as suddenly
as traffic lights
to deer crossings,
frost heaves.

String Quartet, Brooklyn, 1909

Who knows what questions the music answers—
after months of courtship, my grandparents
still nervous, easy only with their instruments,
she nodding approval at her skittering bow

—or is she simply keeping time with the music?
While he leans closer to the cello,
coaxing the deep notes forth,
and somberly shaking his head.

The other players, a young married couple,
watch this quavering, wink
and chase each other up and down
an arpeggio. I like to think of my grandparents

later, sitting on the balcony, hands held,
after the marrieds had caught a carriage home:
neither saying anything for a time,
while inside, in the dimmed parlor,

speechless in their cases, lie violin and cello,
strings taut, perfectly tuned.

A Whaleman to His Wife

My love, I can only hope the good first mate
from the *Charles B. Morgan* has delivered this note
to your sweet hands . . . We crossed
somewhere off Newfoundland, running
the high waters in pursuit of some *rights*,
and set up long enough for one of our boats
to row across with mail, some of it hastily scrawled.
We called out news and exchanged information.
It has been a successful expedition . . .
At night, dear, when a fresh whale
is tied along the hull, and we are in our berths,
the water that sifts in and out of its mouth
makes the beast sound almost alive, breathing!
And when the sharks tug at the carcass
before our deckhands' gaffs
and guns can prick the surface around them,
you would swear the sharks were pulling on
our very beams, on us, as if our hull
and the whale's enormous bulk
together were only of the thinnest skins.
My darling, there is a man named Darwin,
who believes that we, meaning Man,
developed out of fishes, that animals
changed when there were natural forces
pressuring them to do so. It would mean
that we are changing still, that in time,
oh, not in this century or the next,
that these hard berths we sleep in
might be too small for the average-sized man.
All I know is that the smallest bed
grows spacious after a while alone.

The thought of you helps me fall asleep
when the oil lantern swings overhead,
and the breathing begins. Soon
I will be back home, beside you
in our house above the tide.

Shooting at the Sky

I wanted to be like them, my father's friends
sitting around a trash barrel in blood-
stained hunting vests, drinking beer and joking,
cleaning doves that were still warm, the guts
and feathers on their hands. I'd ask my father
for a sip of beer. He always gave me one.

And soon I was like them, standing on the hill
with a shotgun, with my brothers nearby,
each of us under one of the cedars
that our father said were grave markers
from when the plague had swept through Ohio.
("How long ago was that?" I asked. "Cut one down
and count the rings," my father said.)

We waited quietly, watching the sky,
mistaking insects that flew by our faces
for distant doves. I loved the smell
of empty shotgun shells, the smell of oil
on the gun, the gleaming tunnels
of the barrels, like long binoculars,
and the clicking of the safety catch.

We heard gunshots from the other fields,
and then the doves swerved over the treetops,
dodging our shots, their wings pumping
that single flute note through their bodies.
When I hit one, it closed its wings and fell
out of the group, arcing to the ground.

Or, wounded, it flapped down awkwardly,
spiraling, then running. I'd catch it.

One of the last times I went, I grabbed one
by the head, and my hand was suddenly
given the power of flight, flapping wildly,
until the head came off in my hand
and the bird flew into a thicket.

A Connecticut Christmas

A bald alderman eyes the boy in the last pew,
a Jewish boy, visitor from outside the parish,
who imagines his presents perished
and who uses the prie-dieu

for his feet, still chilled from tobogganing.
No one has taken off his coat
in the chill blue church, where vanishing afloat,
holy ghosts of steam drift from fathers breathing.

The boy's friend, disguised in black, enthralled,
incense bobbing like a lure in hand, brings the
    smell of sanctity
to the pucker-mouthed congregants whose density
gives mass and warmth to the fish-cold hall.

The guest meditates in imitation and opens his
    psalter
to any page, any song that will cause
the determined cross-eyes of the alderman to falter
in their cross-eyed stare. If his friend had explained
    the laws

of this Connecticut ritual, the desolation he feels
in the blue-walled echoes would not chase him to
    indulge
his private prayers, his dreams for games, for real
paradise beneath the blue-spruce bulbs.

But he cannot believe what he cannot imagine,
so he tightens his gaze on his neighbor's oration

of snores, which he takes as his lesson of perfect
    serenity
as the hymns diminish to the sermon's eternity

until he, too, sleeps. He wakes to a blur of
    black-stained windows;
everyone has risen, and his friend, in masquerade,
leads a frightening, aisle-swelling mirage parade
of men in black toward the back, trembling rows.

There is no place to hide his shivering ignorance
where the others share the elements of penitence;
he runs out the door through the savage freeze,
from the deepening prayer to the ice-tasseled trees.

On Christmas Eve, he knows no one cries,
so he waits in the snow and bravely pretends
to watch the halo searchlights in the hallowed sky,
and hopes for the happiest holiday of all to end.

M . D . S T E I N

Waterfall

Every spring I walked the newest one
through the woods to Bash Bish Falls
to watch the water, sky-born,
hustle over silt, shock to a halt

across two states, down from Massachusetts
into New York. High from a knurl,
over a knickpoint, the cataract
came through the gorge torrid, curled

like a woman slipping a dress
from her back, smooth-bored
an escarpment and finished vaporous,
mysterious, barely still, adored.

I would think of when I first found
her—shale-fresh, tickled by mist—
before I saw the plungepool down
deep beneath, her hidden negative.

Later I knew she dove without
hesitation, motionless when
I needed her, my head rested
on a riverbed, bulwark against erosion.

High Art

Before the museum, a metallic figure
stood idle in pleasure,
but like mountaineers roped together

he dragged his girls to the gallery,
where children are bored on Sunday,
and in the stylized gossip of the city

drew their attention to his favorite
knight, emblazoned sword and shirt
of mail. His girls preferred to skirt

that chamber, so he clambered up the stairs
to the peaks of civilization, where
the girls' faces bent to hieroglyphs, aware

only of their captivity. "Please don't
make us, please," they pleaded. "Let us play, won't
you?" Their dimples dipped like exclamation
        points.

The nymphs considered a satyr, yawned,
squeaked their sneakers on the marble floor,
made fingers like goggles, giggled and clawed

at their father's pocket until he relented.
Wasted, the art of his opinions, he had at least
        alerted
his girls to genius, but beaten, said, "Survey ahead

and don't get lost!" At a relief he adored
he paused in vigil, then heard the whistle of a
    guard
who gestured out a window, toward the yard.

He left the granite in a hurry,
passed two angels, drunk and happy,
heaven-bound, and then looked down, fatherly.

One had scaled the metallic hull fine,
while her sister skulked below, a philistine,
fingerpainting with mud, creating signs.

Power Lines

I am repeatedly shot and killed while looking
for the misplaced thoughts I dropped here yesterday,
while hoping
to be transported up to the white heights of the
glacier, where it counts. A hippie woman with big bare feet
     and toes
that all point ahead fists up her bread in the plastic shack
     on the
shore. I have missed out on a lot of things, except these
     javelins
of light thrown one after the other out of the hard blue
     mind of the
Kootenays. The dough folds like brains, electrified by
     bready thoughts.
I shoot myself again and again, I am blown away, I rob my
     own banks,
I ambush myself from behind the driftwood thrown up
     here like breast-
works; I turn and am suddenly faced by both barrels,
     throw up my hands
in complete surrender. This is the gun story. Tomorrow
     it will be
knives. Evening stroll; Kootenay Lake. The mind springs
     out of the traps
of caterpillars, fully armed, with wings like spinnakers.

Dreams and Approaches

The voice of dreams maintains that the world will come to
    me even though I
am not sending out teams, hacking my way through this
    world, this jungle
and impenetrable bush. It does come: inch by stone. Leop-
    ard-spotted
birds fall out of the central heavens with the noise of
    trip-hammers, they
plummet into the trefoil with small and innocent crashes.
    This all happens
in the upper pasture. From time to time I become com-
    pletely unimportant.
With immense relief I give up the creation and re-creation
    of the entire
world; of course I could never make it work right, because
    of the details:
the oceans, species, manufacturing belts around the major
    cities, and so on.
At this point someone comes up out of the red shift and
    hands me a train
ticket to Laramie. I will have to speak to the Cattlemen's
    Association
my unique message, and I will take yours with me. Write
    it down. I
promise to speak for both of us, clear and unhindered as
    the dinner bell.
Ring me.

In the Legends

In the legends, it's always like this:
still water, one person alone on a beach,
    oppositions silently sliding
on each other like the two arguments of an
    earthquake,
its inevitable faults.
The mountains move in and out of clouds like
    secret doctrines.
Red willows line up on the sand,
not speaking to one another,
and like this they have spent the night, and the
    morning,
and their entire lives.

After long silences, speech appears
like a voice from a red willow bush, burning:
I love you, or
The bread pans are on that shelf, or
I am afraid of dying.

At one in the morning, poetry fastens
with clean, desperate hands on my nightgown,
saying
Say this, say this, this is
the perfect thing to say.
And then whole lines arrive, whispering modestly
Say me.

Car Doors

A small farm town with a pump in the middle of Main Street, with dogs sitting around the pump waiting for somebody to spill some; the pump has a slick wooden handle. The pickups are parked all up and down the street, and me and Junior and Edna Mae and the rest of the Self kids sit in the back and hold hard on promises of candy. When they finish shopping and if we have been good. Will I get any? I am willing to fight or cheat for it. We sit on the gas cans and observe.

When people walk into the bank, it is with respect and a cleared throat and a nervous thumb on the brass latch. The door of the Blackwater Café is a screen with its wood cut into gingerbread and a scrolly metal handle. They sell ice cream in there. The doors of cars open and women in go-to-town dresses fold into them like egg whites. The door of our pickup is open to keep it cool in the cab and I grab onto the door frame because I am going to climb out, see if you can stop me. Uncle Jimmy comes along with his black hair and killer eyes and slams the pickup door shut on all my fingers.

There are doors that open and reveal more doors. Others shut. Another door opens to the secret doctor's office (nobody goes there anymore but me, with my smashed hand I get this door opened for me) and the old doctor salts my interesting mangled fingers with sulfa drug from a salt shaker. I can't believe how interesting this is. He stole it from the restaurant, they say later. They say more: he was the one they called when the Darling boy was murdered, before there were trucks to have doors to slam on fingers. His office is brown and dark and full of glass cases. My mother hovers around the very old doctor. She seems to seize and hold. Ahead of me is all women's long career with doctors. It will be boring and normal and humiliating, you won't get any orange soda. We begin like this with wounds and afterward even when we are not wounded (when you have babies and when you don't have babies, after you have babies and in between having babies). I see the examining table and, as if by rays, I read from Cute Mom that something is wrong. Strange doctors range in my future, legal and illegal. They will thrust their hands and instruments up my vagina, they will be fully dressed, I won't be, I will just lie there, it will all be normal. All the medical men are waiting for us, clashing their instruments, they think of women as money and car payments, they think of women as doors into which they reach their hands, looking for a career. And Cute Mom hovers anxiously, as if she would protect me from his medicines and no medicines, and his doors, and the doors to hospitals and wards: all the doors that open up after this one door.

In the Saturday sunshine I sit in the back of the pickup like a wounded pup, holding up my bandages, so that the relatives, sorry as hell, and especially Uncle Jimmy, will keep bringing on the Nehi and the ice cream. She'll be sick, says Cute Mom. She'll have to go back to Doc Crean. They immediately stop.

Something has happened and I don't know what it is.

Fifth Grade; or, The Encyclopedia

I approach a school every day, past landscapes and houses I can't recall fifteen minutes afterward. I wear huge dresses of 80 percent polyester and 20 percent cotton, with designs of crushed fried eggs, or maybe they're ruined buildings. My brain is segmented like an ice-cube tray and each segment lasts only so long. I have ten minutes to focus on any one thing and then I go into meltdown. The teacher apparently wants to know what is the major export of Argentina. Doesn't she know? Why is she asking me?

I have no next of kin because I have bought them all tickets to distant places that I found in *The World Book,* and they are not the kind of people who can resist free tickets. Granddad and Lula Belle I have sent to Ulan Bator, under *C.* Mom and Poppa Daddy opted for Acapulco, under *M,* and my sister was given an excursion ticket to Paris, *F.* Elroy got a bus ticket to Mountain Home, Arkansas, a place seen only in brochures put out by Jimmy Driftwood, where he can shoot squirrels and play pinochle in the secret backrooms of his mind.

I have sent them off special delivery, to flat places in colored half-tone photographs (the women wearing handkerchiefs in wild designs as if they wore their hearts on their heads, their inarticulate, smiling husbands holding market packages or riding down on boars, they are Circassian or Bantu, and behind them the bluish mountains play tones on the observer's soul. Solitude. Excursions), and so they are stamped with goodbye kisses and mailed off into *The World Book.*

. . .

I continue to live in the house we abandoned the last time we moved. There are a few things they forgot: three jelly glasses, a high-topped tennis shoe, and there is a drawer lined with newspaper for the knives and forks and spoons, and in it are two parakeet eggs. The newspaper in the drawer says the Slater grain elevator burnt down and Judy Canova is playing at the Sunset Theater. The sun rises out of the Mississippi and sets in western Kansas. Out in the daytime world mysterious normal people walk through shock waves.

Far away are the songs of chickens. The yard is full of petunias and morning glories, butterflies elevate like aftermaths, bits of wallpaper and insulation scattered in the still central air after the explosion. They are graceful and slow, unlike family life, and drift onto morning glories, now folded like gloves.

The World Book has a clumsy, distracted, and episodic devotion to truth, eager under the maroon covers, wanting to be of use; like an eyewitness at civilization's five-car pileup, it offers everything it knows. The perihelion of Mercury is sometimes 36 million miles from the sun, Geronimo died in 1909, and yes! the capital of Argentina is Buenos Aires. In the stillness my mind drifts onto the morning glories, now folded like hands.

But suddenly the family begins to re-emerge, it's unfair, everybody has their dream time even in the middle of evacuations, but all of a sudden they are reappearing under the most bizarre headings, *P* for psychology, *M* for myth, the self-absorbed gods and goddesses dressed in bedsheets, sandals, the impossible Demeter grieving,

Icarus who burnt and fell, repeating themselves like sales slips.

They have all moved to a town beside the Mississippi, while I have floated sideways in the mind. It is time to go back and inhabit the body's unforgiving house; move on to puberty. Bottles will sparkle and fester in some deep basement, Poppa Daddy will march fearlessly into riverfront taverns, trading used cars with the river bargemen, he will fight and shout and have fun. The only thing left to do before I go back to reality is to make a heading under *Individual* and enter myself there under *I,* write my own section for future reference, and slowly close the doors of the book after me. This encyclopedia includes, after all, *Ethics* as well as *Elizabeth I* and *Eclipse.*

(look at the black sun's raving white corona!), and here in my mother's house thirty-two years later I discover again Athena in all her improbable armor, Austria's blue mountains, the inner workings of telephones; all the world's false splendor and innocence, which displays its fifth-grade magic as the high-quality stock slides out of my hands.

Everybody Knew but Gave Different Answers

All that remains from the work of Skopas
are the feet. Sometimes not even that.
Only irregularities on the plinth which may
indicate how they were placed. Learned men
argue (using the feet or shadows of feet
and the exact diagrams of German professors)
about what the arms were doing and the quality
of the sculpture. As we do with our lives.
Deciding what the woman is like according
to whether she truly was happy when it rained
all that day. If her dead father was
the ambassador and whether she really came
or just wanted to please. Deciding the years
to come from the feet and the academics,
when we could listen to Linda's heart
in the summer nights season after season.
Winnow with Michiko years of foggy mornings
in San Francisco. Taking time. Making sure.

Looking Away from Wanting

On Fish Mountain she has turned away
from the temple where they painted
pictures of Paradise everywhere inside,
so a population who prayed only
not to live could imagine yearning.
She is looking at a tree instead.
Below is the place where the man
and the beautiful woman will eat cold
noodles almost outside on a hot day.
And below that the sound of fast water
with a barefoot woman beside it beating
an octopus on the wet stones. And then
the floor of the valley opening out on
the yellow of mustard blooming and smoke
going straight up from huge farmhouses
in the silent early evening. Where they
will walk through all of it slowly,
easy, not talking much. A small him
and a smaller her with long black hair,
so happy together beginning the trip
toward where she will die and leave him
tenderly looking at the back of her
turned away looking at a small tree.

Going Wrong

The fish are dreadful. They are brought up
the mountain in the dawn most days, beautiful
and alien and cold from night under the sea,
the grand rooms fading from their flat eyes.
Soft machinery of the dark, the man thinks,
washing them. "What do you know of machinery?"
the Lord says. Sure, the man says quietly
and cuts into them, laying back the dozen struts,
getting at the muck of something terrible.
"You are the one who chooses to live this way,"
the Lord says. "I built cities where things
are human. I made Italy and you go to Greece."
He washes away the blood and arranges the fish
prettily on a big plate. Starts the onions
in the hot olive oil and puts in peppers.
"You have started to live without women!"
He takes everything out and puts in the fish.
"No one knows where you are. People forget you.
You are vain and stubborn." The man slices
his tomatoes and lemons. Takes out the fish
and scrambles eggs. I am not stubborn, the man
    says,
laying it on the table in the walled courtyard
and early sun, the shadows of swallows flying
on the food. I am not stubborn, I am greedy.

Man Walking Down the Mountain
Alone in the Morning

The cuckoo on the other side of the pretty valley
sings and he repeats the song inside. Cuckoo.
Knowing that for the Elizabethans it meant
what your wife had done with another man.
He thinks of Michiko and hopes she is unfaithful,
beautiful and delicate making love with the Devil
in the muggy room behind his shabby office
as he explains that Hell was already a slum
when he got the job, Buicks burning in the dark
along the highways. The Devil explaining
he was not the one who did the judging
and sending weak people down into the lakes
of molten lead. He likes to think of the Devil
feeding her lemons to help with the heat.
Holding shaved ice in his mouth before sucking
softly at her sweating nipples to make her glad.

1953

All night in the Iowa café. Friday night
and the farm boys with their pay.
Fine bodies and clean faces. All of them
proud to get drunk. No meanness,
just energy. At the next table they talked
cars for hours, friends coming and going,
hollering over. The one with the heavy face
and pale hair kept talking of the Chevy
he had three years ago and how it could
take anything in second. Wasn't that true?
Fucking right. Moaning that he should never
have sold it. Didn't he show old Ev?
Bet your ass! That Fourth of July
when Shelvadeen got too much patriotism
and beer and gave some to everybody
down by the river. Ev so mad because
I left him like he was standing still
that he didn't get any. Best car that ever
was and never should have let it go,
he said, tears falling on his eggs.

What the Viscount Saw

I was born under the old sky.
We were poor that year,
and ever after,
and offered no entertainments.
Poverty made us
see things differently:
my father began
to put his feet on the table

and my aunt, my mother's sister,
spurned the viscount,
my father's only friend,
and fell in love
with Monsieur Amiel,
my preceptor,
who went mad with joy.
He died. She died.
They were buried together
in a grave sheeted with lilies.

The viscount still came
each day and stood
by the hearth, laughing
and waving his hands,
a candlestick in one
and a wineglass in the other,
painting a thousand airy visions
for my father's amusement

but telling me
I would love a woman one day
more than I loved

my own strength and beauty,
and she would be out of reach;
as he spoke,
I could feel the afternoon
closing around his heart.

Now we are three:
me, my father,
who sits before the fire
with his hat on,
and my mother,
who has never ceased
to love him
or to joke
about his bad manners.

DAVID KIRBY

Crustacea

> Darwin's study of barnacles extended over
> eight years, 1846 to 1854. In his systematic
> way of working he generally set aside two
> and a half hours each day for the barnacles.
> This became so much a part of the family
> routine that one of his children assumed that
> this was what grownup men did and asked the
> children of another household, "When does
> your father do his barnacles?"

—George Gaylord Simpson, *The Book of Darwin*

THE NEIGHBOR'S ELDEST CHILD

Our father does his barnacles in a somewhat irregular manner, devoting himself to them for hours on end and then allowing two weeks or more to pass without giving them so much as a glance. But though he does not do them nearly so well as Mr. Darwin does his, nonetheless he takes such pleasure in his studies that we not only indulge but emulate his example, though we prefer quoits and pitchpenny to shellfish. By "our" I mean the father of the nine of us, including Charlotte and Edward, deceased.

THE NEIGHBOR OBSERVED

No, no, no. Hmmm . . . ahhh . . . I—hmmm . . . no . . . I wonder . . . yes . . . I . . . ahh, that's . . . hmmmmmm . . . blast!

CHARLOTTE AND EDWARD, LOOKING DOWN
ON THEIR FATHER'S EXERTIONS

We have learned with regret that, in the process of doing his barnacles, our father has lost his traditional beliefs, becoming a non- but not clearly an anti-Christian, from there passing through a period of non-Christian theism, and ending in a nearly but not completely atheistic agnosticism. We neither complain nor disapprove, though we regret that he does not share our view or expect confidently to enjoy an immortal afterlife with us.

We died young, by which time we had absorbed, at our mother's knee, a belief in the hereafter as perdurable as the chalk flats on which our father's house is situated. Perhaps it is well that we did not live to do our barnacles as he does his, for the doing of them would have knocked our belief on the head, and clearly it is our belief that has brought us to this most pleasant place.

THE SONG OF THE BARNACLES

Pauvre us!
We are the order Cirripedia
and kin to all barnacles,
yet different

from those of Darwin
because *nous ne savons pas*
when we are going
to be studied.

For Darwin's lot,
it's clockwork:
two and a half hours
each day.

How know we this?
Très simple:
Their brine
is our brine.

THE NEIGHBOR'S WIFE, BUT NOT WITHOUT BITTERNESS

For some months there was a serving girl who would sit on my husband's lap and kiss him, but that was all. She seemed baffled by the things he hissed at her: his raptures, his declarations of devotion, his promises to divorce me and take her away to Italy. I knew and said nothing. Eventually she became frightened and ran away. He turned to science. Though his research is fitful, I must say he is trying very hard. Everyone should have a hobby.

THE NEIGHBOR'S ELDEST CHILD AGAIN

Let's face it, these are nervous times. Small wonder that Mr. Dickens, up in London, and after him Mr. Robert Louis Stevenson, will grow rich from their pen portraits of the divided self. Here at home the emphasis is on being sensible and not running out to play until your dinner goes down. A boy at school says his aunt threatened to punish him by hanging his cat. The constable came, but most of the townspeople say this was an overreaction; the cat scratched the aunt and ran beneath the sofa, where he has been ever since. Also, I don't notice anyone going out of his way to answer *my* questions.

Knowledge

Richard Nixon,
Richard Nixon,
selling papers,
bruised and legless,
from a cart,
watching the sky
with one crazed eye,
fearing the birds;
I know your heart.

DadDick

It's a made-up name, and no one knows now
what the sound of it once was—
DeSantis, D'Allessandro maybe—something
with a Latin coloration, to look at him.

Walking block after block after dinner
it would happen on occasion
that we would gain access to benches,
but he never did tell me the truth of things.

I'd ask about his family and then
he'd be angry and raving about what bums
poor people are—how they just want a free ride
and to drag you down to their level.

He'd put half a continent between himself
and them, just as they had once put an ocean
        between.
I think he was great as a young guy—mined gold,
raced motorcycles, sold washing machines
and Cadillacs all over Texas.

But when he got old he got depressed,
gave a lot of money to the Church,
would sit around complaining
that there wasn't anything anywhere
that wasn't exactly like
everything else.

When I turned twenty-one
he looked at me with tears
in his eyes and said I looked exactly
like his sister, Rose.
I never saw her, though.

Today I Saw My Child

Today I saw my child
floating down over the lake,
shimmering in the light,
coming down to rest on the water.
Turning her face to me,
I saw she was the burst seed
of a dandelion, the soft stuff of a weed.
She floated on the water,
the green water,
my daughter floated on the water.
I thought I heard her singing,
though it may have been
the light, or the breeze,
or the silent sound the water makes
when it translates for the child,
saying, "Look, Father, I am everywhere.
You can touch me.
I am not lost."

We Paint the Future

Almost no one in them.
If it looks as if it flies two continents, it must be the
    right kind of thing.
It is encapsulating it for the sake of whatever sake.
I'm a lumper rather than a splitter.
Split when you need it, lump it until you need it.
All right, Susan's horses.
Unbelievable; it's like a store.
After all you think about, are you going to give a
    tree to the orphanage?
Are you going to plant a bush in Brazil, or
    something like that?
But it's not a big household name.
But it perceives as something else.
And the supply is a reflection of the bodywork.
As of right now, it's maybe, maybe I'm just
    impatience.

Sleeping with Bears

Okay, so I've written my poem about
going to bed with stuffed bears and
it goes like this:

It's easier to sleep with a bear
than a man because
he lies in the curve
of your arm,
a plush brown comfort,
and never says a word.

He tangles in your flannel
nightgown unperturbed
and does not say a single word.

Tumbling out of bed, he waits,
patient as a back porch,
till shattered dawn
when you awake
and someone else has gone.

That's my bear poem.
But don't be too sure
about believing in
my bear poem,
you
in your plush brown overcoat.

America

I went through
old things today,
cleared away my daughter
for my son.
They're from two wives,
two lives, identical
since nothing repeats itself.
They seemed so different
they had to be the same.

She's twenty, her shoes
and the stars they go to
in another world.
He's three. He's where
I eat and sleep
and hide myself.
You could say he's my home.
A scholar of slams,
I'm careful how I
close and open doors.
I leave but these windows
open, so much no more,
and let things get
just so out of hand
they're at every finger's edge.
I am known
as the perfect homemaker.
Like the smart pig, I say,
he is all bricks.
Like mad Mrs. Winchester
he will not stop building.

I shelved her books
three years above his bed
to dance his sleep
to my own wooden
dream of permanence,
unhinge me from its loss.
I never thought
how they could drop
on his roof
like a demolition ball,
on his name
like a world of ink.

Putting her books
away for his,
I found a small
jeweler's box of gold:
a college ring
with a lofted stone,
a wedding band, faceted,
a ring engraved with his initials,
the only profit
from my grandfather's death,
the adjustment for his
shrinking finger
perfect for mine,
not yet full-fleshed.
M.S., a world in those two letters
blotted by my own.
One thing falls to another.
The clouds, as my son said,

seeking his own replacements,
eat the stars.
The books will fade
into his fingers.

My grandfather's ring
was a gift from his clean-
faced father
to celebrate his arrival
in America.
Welcome to America.

Veterans

We were in the living room
with Milton Berle
to his neck and fully clothed
in a tank of water
this room's size,
and we were laughing:
my mother, whose flesh
had just begun to fall,
and I, and I was ten.
The Second War was done,
the boys, as they were
named, were home,
but store-bought stars
hung in their windows still.
My mother laughed so much
I almost flew.
Wound like a caterpillar
in the knot of her chest,
only he, one hour
each Tuesday night, could break
to set me free, I was always
deep in love with need.

Tires burned against the tar,
fenders thudded like a late-night
stranger at the door.
My mother's face widened
everywhere, smoothed
to youthfulness by fear.
Springing from the stiff
stick chair beside my softer one,
she held one breast as though

on the long way to the window
it might fall,
knotted like a kerchief
to the sinking stone of her heart.
I kept my place and
watched her eyes and
heard as she returned
the words she reached for
with memory through breath.
I thought it was you, she said,
and though I laughed and said,
But I'm right here,
on the corner where we
lived and forces met,
under the streetlight
of the ratios of power,
the patient vengeance of the gods,
it might have been.

On every street in the neighborhood,
while veterans hawked melons
from their carts,
once vivid stars
grayed in the windows
to keep such vehicles apart.

Decatur Cemetery

I was struck less by the gravestones
in the field through which I passed
than by the manner of three squirrels

who had toppled over a clay pot
of yellow roses, crushed the blossoms,
begun to nibble on their petals

and who, as I passed by, dashed behind
the gravestone of a colonel who served
Georgia and died in one of the wars.

Vermeer's Head of a Girl

[I]

This girl with a gold earring
unravels her blue turban
one century at a time

with pink camels casting
a shadow on pyramids
in a pastel beside her.

She is the silent poetry
of color on white canvas,
but I will paint her black

cover all her colors
even the milk in her eyes
that washes down my throat.

[II]

Whole nights pass without touching.
I sometimes sleep on the last look
wrapped in blue blankets, thinking too much.

She breathes with Arabian rhythm and stares
with Latin morals, saying nothing at all.
Now she looks at the cat asleep on a stack

of journals, at the wall where a family
portrait hangs, and in the doorway
where another woman stands.

She has been quiet for three centuries.
Breathing, I breathe without life.
I wait endlessly for her to speak.

[III]

I will live out this love:
bear no trace of her kiss.

She spent six months in Paris
and knows what is her due.

The cracks are already there
in the white paint of her eyes.

Vuillard

Lips brought to a point, a whole spring
spent with one wife in a French parlor
and a potent theory of color.

She hides among apricots and blues,
raspberry and paper-white stripes of a dress
blending with the books.

And his self-portrait presents him
as it should, his hair leaf-yellow,
his eyes bloodshot, behind him black.

Three centuries earlier in the same country
Montaigne would write, "I play the child.
I cannot endure myself."

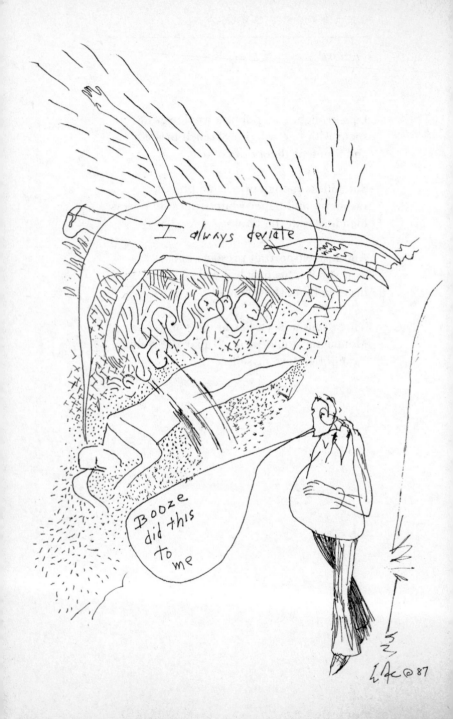

We go to visit one of Peter's friends again. A film director. He and Peter are deep in a conversation in which I should be able to participate but can't. They're not discussing IBM PCs or the RBIs in the 1956 World Series. They're saying something about enunciating a response to the backlash of liberal guilt.

I have to get out of my chair. I could walk around the high-rise apartment reading bookshelves if I knew this man, which I don't, which is usually the case with Peter's friends.

The only place I can think of to go is to the bathroom—sit on the pot for a few minutes and look at my pretty Pucci underwear if there are no *Playboy*s to read. Check myself out in the mirror, try to cry a little.

I open the medicine cabinet, find birth-control pills, Valium, Preparation H. The pharmacy labels are from Schwab's; the price sticker on the deodorant says FedMart. Pull open the shower to see what kind of shampoo this film director uses—Pantene for Men or Prell. The shampoo's from Aunt Tilly's Health Food Emporium—Ph-balanced Jhirmack, quivering like orange Jell-O. See if it's drugstore or department-store cologne he buys; Max Factor or something French. See where he stashes the blow dryer. Take off my shoes and weigh myself. It's the director's hair dryer I love the best.

The towels are so thick—forest-green with chrome-yellow stripes—the tiles so clean. I'm going to take off my clothes and get into the shower. Stand under the hot water in this warm, plush, bachelor bathroom.

You with the good shampoo, real wool carpets, and brown wallpaper with horses bucking on it, you must have a maid in your shower every day, and you worry about being bald. You must be old, but I can't tell how old.

There is a red light for heat, which makes the bathroom

look, strangely, red. I am really in a balloon. I've been saying bathroom but what I meant to say was balloon. A red balloon.

I look pretty here, it is such a nice dress. I feel like a gracious hostess. This lushness is my dress, my hostess gown, this perfectly decorated room of my own. Would you boys care to join me for a little gin-and-tonic on this hot summer afternoon?

I don't want to go outside. It's much too nice here in my red bathroom, surrounded by bottles of elegance. I don't want to go back to my leather chair and stare out the window at the city lights.

Hello, boys. I shall return wet and smelling of Paco Rabanne *Pour Homme.* Peter will explain that I do this often; he'll be charmed. We shall smile fondly at each other, join hands lightly, and continue the conversation like one nicely linked couple. The director will think we are in love.

Hello, boys. I'll go back to the living room and they'll still be talking. I'll take my chair by the coffee table and drink vodka and chew ice cubes and finish all the barbecued soybeans in the Steuben-glass bowl.

My hair is still wet. I follow a hallway lined with photographs of the director shaking hands with astronauts that leads back to where they all are. **Q**

I used to have an unusually strong love for my sister Ruth, partly because I protected her when she was twenty-four and I was seven years old. She was married to a mulatto Haitian who thought beating her up was a good way to work off tension from a day of real estating.

I have a vivid memory of one time in particular, because it was the one time I saw her try to get away, and it was the first time I tried to save her; it wasn't the last for me.

I was at her home being baby-sat when he came in once and they started to fight. He slapped her—and the next thing I knew, she was out the door and he was first calling and then running after her. I looked for a likely place to crawl under, and happened to glance at the tin sheriff's star pinned to my breast. What the hell kind of a sheriff am I? I thought, accusing myself.

They came back together, he carrying her from behind, she kicking the door open with her bare feet. I noticed that her foot was bleeding between her big toe and the next, where he had stepped his heel in. The color of the blood and the nail polish didn't match—it was Fire Engine Red—and maybe this detail has also helped perpetuate a strange predilection I have for older women's feet.

I told him I'd arrest him if he didn't leave my sister alone. He told me to butt out.

That's the way it stood until she left him, and then there were other messes she got into, and me trying to help. I've always gone for older women, maybe because there was something absent in my relationship with my sister, or maybe because there was too much.

"I'll give you anything, Michael," Ruth said, "except sex."

"Why not?" I asked.

"Because I'm your sister," she said.

But she should have been as astonished at her statement as at my follow-up.

That's long in the past. When I called Karen and told her to meet me at the station in White Plains, I hadn't planned on staying for long. I took some things along for the weekend —in case it went that far—and went to Grand Central.

A week earlier, I was lying on the sofa with Karen. She was on her back, lightly caressing my ankle with her toes. She looked like she was going to tell me something unpleasant, which she didn't want me to take too hard.

She'd found another job and was moving to White Plains.

I took it damn hard and stopped listening altogether. I don't know why I felt it had to be the end, because White Plains is only an hour away from New York City by train. But Karen wasn't talking to a pinhead, and I knew she knew she didn't have to spell things out.

I remember lying there trying to hold on to the feeling of intimacy. How she used to put her stockings on in front of me. How cool I was when I was in her room. And then I thought there's no point in getting sentimental.

I always found it pretty easy to meet older women, although they didn't often sleep with me. Mostly, I met them in laundromats or even at the park with their little kids. My first lover was my eighth grade English teacher.

She was a young woman, but nine years older than me, and that was a lot. She was thin and had a haughty manner in class. What got me from the start were her high heels. Some days she wore a high-heeled pump with a small hole over the big toe. Her toenail had a classic shape, and you could spy one red oval surrounded by black leather shoe. Perfect!

Apart from that, she was ordinary, and flat chested. Most fourteen year olds are idiots about that; most of my friends talked about Stephanie Bergen, and they probably dreamt about our physics teacher, too—only they were too chicken to admit it.

I stayed in school late one afternoon, and five minutes before I knew she'd want to leave I went to Mrs. Klein's room and started a complicated discussion about who remembers what topic in Tolkien's *The Lord of the Rings.* Predictably, Mrs. Klein didn't want to stay longer than she had to, and offered me a lift part of the way home so we could finish our talk.

In her car, I barely listened or spoke. It was an almost ecstatic ride as I watched her feet manipulate the pedals. She asked impatiently—perhaps it was the tenth time she'd asked already—"Michael, where can I drop you?"

She left me off at an underpass on Queens Boulevard near her access to the Long Island Expressway. Queens Boulevard was a wide boulevard with fast-food chains, an Elks Lodge, and an AFL-CIO local. Alexi and I once went in to ask them if we could borrow their copy of the Communist Manifesto. The receptionist smiled and put down her book; we bolted out without waiting for an answer. We thought nothing was funnier than assaulting unsuspecting middle-class matrons.

I also went door-to-door with Alexi, selling bogus orders for hedgehogs. My pitch was that they're nice on the sofa and a handy conversation piece. Twenty-five dollars C.O.D. I got one order.

Hunting for crazy snapshots, I once found a dead German shepherd under that underpass where Mrs. Klein dropped me off. I got Alexi to pose next to it; he was good. He lay on his back with his arms and legs straight up in the air. I called it "Two Dead Dogs."

So much for childhood adventures.

Mrs. Klein must have been out of her mind. I said no one would be home and she believed me. How she could trust a kid my age is beyond me.

It was difficult the first time. I found I couldn't get hard, much less get off, without a toe in my mouth. I made the whole procedure complicated and gymnastic, and it wasn't worth all the effort. But what did I know?

The next time, Mrs. Klein seemed to know what I wanted.

"Take your pants off," she ordered.

She lifted her dress over her head, and kept her bra, red panties, and pumps on.

"Is this what you want?"

"Yeah," I croaked.

She pointed her foot at me and said, "Lick it with the shoe on."

I licked the smooth red varnish on the big toe, and then the instep laced with thin blue veins. Then I took off her shoe.

"I know just what you want," she said, wiggling her toes just out of reach of my lips.

When the school year ended, there was a dance that all the teachers were invited to. Mrs. Klein came with her husband. He was a short, broad redhead with freckles. I hated him instantly, and kept away from her all night. I imagined that he beat her every night, and that I had to rescue her.

At home that night, I composed a poem for her begging her to leave her husband and live with me. I never heard from her again.

The next year I was in high school, and I fell in love with the senior class president. Her father was the Italian ice magnate of Queens. I called her up and told her, "You don't know me, but my name is Michael, and I'd like to go out with you. Maybe you've seen me in the halls?"

"No," she said.

I went back to older women.

Again, I have to stress that most of them didn't sleep with me, and I could tell why. I had a lot of pimples, plus I was under eighteen, so they couldn't take me everywhere they wanted—like Studio 54, for instance.

You might ask, well, then why would they want to be with you? Couldn't they play with someone their own age?

No, no, they couldn't. Have you ever bothered to consider the choices women have? If height were given out in the same proportion as brains, most men would be able to roller-skate under Dunkin Donut counter stools. I ask you, how could they pass me up?

Even when I didn't get to sleep with them, it was an even trade as far as I was concerned. I was a good listener, which was good for them, and I was a good listener because I loved to listen. I found out stuff it takes most people fifteen years to learn, if they learn it at all.

The first time I saw Karen Booziak I was with her older sister, who had just moved into our building.

Rosy was thin and flat chested, and had very little going for her upstairs. But being the bundle of sexed-up nerves that I was, she was a hippie goddess.

In exchange for beers and conversation, I sandpapered her kitchen table until my knuckles were too raw to continue.

I say conversation. With someone like Rosy it was easy. She was probably almost twice my age.

With girls my own age, it was impossible. People say don't worry, it'll come naturally—but people usually say a pack of lies.

The one time I actually went on a date with a girl, it was raining. We talked about the pizza, homework, what teachers we hated in common, and then I walked her home. I wasn't even bright enough to walk under the same umbrella with her. No good-bye kiss, nothing. I didn't do that again.

But I was always a hit with older women. No one in my family likes anyone else, and that's always a good conversation starter. No one would believe half the stuff was true, so I have to water it down a little.

For instance, I never say my older brother is in jail for being a con artist (the truth). People would think I'm a liar. So I tell them he's in jail for murder, and they eat it right up.

I have a sister in California my dad threw out of the house because she cursed out my mother. I tell people he threw her out for hooking.

So you can see I don't have problems finding things to say. People say I'm mature for my age after they hear that stuff. What they really mean is that it's a miracle I'm not in some psycho ward downtown. They get the idea I've learned a lot or grown a lot in some ways because my life is interesting. But none of this stuff is happening to me as much as I wish it was. It's happening to them, my family. It only affects me subtlely. It depresses me somewhat. I wouldn't dare tell any of my pals, which is why all these older women are perfect for me.

I didn't like Karen at first. Maybe because she was younger than her sister—probably around twenty-one, though I never found out for sure.

She came in wearing blue sunglasses and tripping her brains out. She had to get together with their parents in a few hours, so Rosy brought some coke out of a drawer to help get her straight. Karen was more over-and-out than anyone I'd ever seen.

The coke is how I found out Rosy already had a boyfriend —a coke dealer. That's when I decided to focus on Karen instead.

She moved in with Rosy that fall and went to Queens Community College, majoring in psych. I was really bowled over because she was so bright.

I remember those days as my coke and Joni Mitchell days, because that's all we ever did together. We spent a lot of time in threes. But that changed when Karen got her own place in Astoria.

Karen wore a lot of denim the days when we first met, but that was something else which also changed once she started working full-time. I thought it was a change for the better. But Karen had flexible values. They changed depending on the circumstances.

It turned out that Karen already had a boyfriend, too. But I didn't find out about him until I was already in love with her. The worst of it was he wasn't a hateable guy. His name was Larry, and he was in the Merchant Marines; he was away a lot.

Karen was working as a receptionist in a fashion designer's showroom. She told me everything they say about men in the fashion world is true—they're all gay.

She was frustrated, and I commiserated with her, but I found it depressing that as long as she was going to be unfaithful to Larry, she couldn't do that with me.

I stayed over at her apartment often, and that impressed my friends enough. My mother was cool about it. In fact, my mother kind of cheered me on. My father wasn't too happy, but he was helpless. He went along with anything my mother wanted, except if she wanted him to forgive her foulmouthed daughter.

One of those nights, Karen told me she wasn't ready to fuck me yet. I hung around anyhow, not because I was patient, but because I had nothing better cooking.

I had to put up with some incredible bullshit. One of the side effects of being the harmless, sensitive guy was that sometimes I almost didn't exist as a man at all.

As an example, I drag out Karen's friend Sherry. She always wore sandals and a muddy-red nail polish. But she was a royal pain in the ass.

One night she came over fairly late while Karen and I were smoking pot and listening to the Grateful Dead. I was pissed at the sudden intrusion, because Karen and I were on the sofa and you never know.

Sherry was all in a snit because of (who else) her boyfriend, who thankfully I never met. God knows what atrocities he had committed in the past, but this night he had gone beyond the pale!

For the next hour, they cursed and groaned—Sherry cried, and Karen with her out of sympathy, and they played this song by Gloria Gaynor, "I Will Survive," which is about a woman who won't take her ex-lover back after he left her, because he was a bastard, and she found out she didn't need him anyhow. That's all well and good, but they played it fifteen times, and sang along and danced around and cursed men and all their ways.

And here's the crucial thing—at one point Karen turned to me and said, "Don't worry, we're not mad at you, you don't really count."

Sherry eventually broke up with her boyfriend (temporarily), and Karen thought it might be a good idea if I went out with her. I told Karen I didn't care about Sherry at all but that I wouldn't mind sleeping with her. The only objection I had was that Karen might change her mind about me, but I'd be with Sherry and Karen wouldn't want to fuck up her women's solidarity-let's-never-fight-over-a-man-because-they're-not-worth-it thing. Karen told me not to worry about it.

Sherry turned out to not be interested in me, but she was a worthless pinhead, and it pissed me off like hell whenever she came up in conversation.

Meanwhile Karen was still desperate because Larry was away. She was even going out at night with her faggy friends from the designer showroom.

One fine Saturday night we met them at eleven-thirty at a disco called P.T. Barnum's Ringling Room. Karen warned me in advance that it was a mixed place, including a lot of drag queens who really looked like women. And we were on our own once inside the joint.

I had met Rudy before, but none of the other guys. All of

them were thin, tall, and balding—Rudy most of all. I felt awkward in my best polyester shirt, which Rudy informed me was one season out of style.

Karen was wearing a red dress cut down deep, dazzlingly high red heels, and red toenail polish. I had never remembered her looking so good. I hoped like hell the whole damn place was gay.

It wasn't, and she was off in a corner doing poppers with a curly-haired geek she eventually gave her phone number to. Though she didn't sleep with him that night, the idea of it was probably enough to keep her satisfied.

Too bad.

There were three floors to P.T.'s, so I decided to get lost. The third floor was really nothing more than a balcony from which you could watch naked trapeze artists hang on to each other at eye level. The second floor was where you could watch them from below, through the holes in the net. I wasn't used to drinking as much as I was and got plastered fairly quickly. As a result, I couldn't keep my head tilted to watch them for very long, and wandered in search of a woman instead.

Somehow Rudy found me up there, and must have watched me for a while. I'd been eyeing the most gorgeous woman I'd ever seen while nonchalantly supporting a Greek column with my shoulder. Rudy came up as I was answering a smile with one of my own, and said, "Isn't that the most heavenly queen?"

I looked up at him, and he nodded and smiled. To this day I'm not absolutely convinced, but I took his word for it. He cupped my ass with his hand and asked me to dance.

I declined.

"You'll never know till you try," he said.

He smiled again and went away. I thought he was kind, and almost reconsidered.

I found Karen downstairs; she was as drunk as I was and the poppers had worn off, so she was tired, too. The curly-haired guy was nowhere in sight. Rudy and his friends decided to go to a male only after-hours place, so Karen and I took a cab back to Astoria.

"Rudy said for you to call him if you ever change your mind," she said in the cab.

Karen told me she'd given her number to that guy, and I was really upset.

"What about Larry?" I cried.

"What about him? He's gone for three more months."

"But he'll be back," I said.

"People change a lot," Karen said. "He's probably changed. I've changed. We're not the same people anymore. We probably won't even like each other anymore."

It was drunken drivel and I knew it. But I was hurt anyhow. I felt it all referred to me obliquely, and I hadn't changed, that was for sure. I was still loyal. Her theory scared me because I didn't understand it; it was beyond my experience. I felt attacked and betrayed. I argued with her all the way back. About how love doesn't die, how people don't really change essentially—they just evolve. God knows why I argued, because this was the news I was waiting for. With Larry out of the way, I could move in as the permanent boyfriend.

Inside her apartment, she got the spare sheets out and plopped them on the sofa as usual. I was almost in tears; she was furious with me. She went into her room and closed the door.

"Karen, we've got to straighten this out," I said.

I couldn't bear the thought of going to sleep with her mad at me.

"Get away from my door," she said.

"Karen, please," I insisted.

She said, "Don't force yourself like this Michael, goddamn it. I have the right to not argue in my own house. Get that through your head."

"At least say good night," I sobbed.

"Good night," she said through the closed door.

. . .

I set up my bedding, allowing the tears to roll, and then cried loudly; I wanted to force her to come out to me out of pity. But she must have fallen asleep instantly.

I woke up to the smell of coffee and nail-varnish remover in the morning.

The curly-haired guy didn't turn out to be anything important, but he was good in bed, she said. I always got the details from Karen. She was always into drooling, and anyone who couldn't get into it was out. She liked to drool her drool into the guy's mouth, and have him drool it back—hers or his, it didn't matter. She liked the spit to ooze out from between their mouths while they kissed. She liked having her tits, legs, face, lubricated, she said, with a coat of spit.

Apparently, the curly-haired guy was a good drooler.

I envied him.

And then Karen moved away. Away from her gay showroom, away from New York, away from Astoria, and up to White Plains.

When I got off the train at White Plains, there wasn't any Karen at the station. Maybe she thought I was on the next train. Every time one pulled in, I figured Karen thought that was the one I was in, and she'd show up to pick me up. I was mad at her, but at the same time I knew that the second I'd see her, my anger would disappear. It's always that way with people I love. I'm so glad to see them finally that I forget they kept me waiting so damn long.

There wasn't any shade in the parking lot, which was where I was waiting. I lost patience, and decided to find her place on my own. I went on foot, and it didn't matter because I was glad to feel sorry for myself.

Karen didn't get home till late in the evening, and when she did, she had a guy wearing a checkered shirt and cords in tow. He had well-cared-for shoulder-length hair and looked rich in a suburban way.

"Hell, Mike, I forgot," Karen said.

She said she was real happy to see me, but it had slipped her mind until late, and then she guessed I'd gone back to Queens. She even seemed a little miffed because I was being puppy doggish.

Shit, I thought, isn't that what she had me around for?

I couldn't stand it anymore. I let myself get halfheartedly invited in for a cup of coffee. I could see this guy was nice enough but that he was also hot for me to leave. I took my time with the coffee and then hit Karen up for a loan. I knew I'd never see her again, and this was my way of telling her. She didn't have much cash, so the guy said he'd loan me some. That was fine. He loaned me sixty just to make sure it was enough, and my only regret was that he probably wasn't going to make her pay it back.

I thought it'd be just the thing to do, to take a Greyhound bus as far as I could. When I found out that was exactly Pough-keepsie, I said to hell with that.

Sixty bucks was plenty enough dough for killing a weekend and a memory without having to live off cat food. Then I won ten bucks at a church festival craps game, and that helped, too.

I didn't think about a hell of a lot, which is one way of forgetting. I found a paper and checked to see how the Yan-kees were doing. I realized I hadn't paid any attention to them in years.

My parents were pretty worried, and they had the entire New York State police force out looking for me. I can just picture my father assuming the command post, shoving peo-ple left and right.

It wasn't until I was in the White Plains prowl car on my way to the police station, and was trying to decide what I was going to tell my parents, that I even thought about Karen again.

Things occur suddenly, but a lot happens first. One min-ute you're in love, then you're not. People move on without the slightest hesitation. **Q**

[I]

Eat my fuck, someone yelled from on top. Who's that, I wondered, and what to do next. Everything means something. If it wasn't for Eleanor, I'd never have been here. Eat my fuck! I was beginning to, all right. And I had not even known her one week.

Who can say their lives have changed in fifteen minutes? I can and I know it. Believe me, Eleanor wasn't very special. I meet women usually that way. Who's that, I thought when I first saw her. It is an agonizing process, meeting women, and getting them into bed. Not with Eleanor. What does "eat my fuck," even when you think about it, really mean?

Everything means something. In my life, few things this exceptional have taken place. And everything *does* mean something, and if it wasn't for Eleanor, I'd not be here. —Listen, there is a fine line between human sexuality. But with Eleanor you crossed it. Eat my fuck was now beginning to enter my life. And as it did, I joined invisibly with it.

[II]

The next morning we were married on a flight to Las Vegas. Eleanor couldn't wait and ended up drunk and got the pilot. He was obliging. She could always get whatever she wanted from men. I was beginning to see that, all right. Who can say that their lives have changed in fifteen minutes? I was married accordingly to the plainest woman God had ever set upon this planet. Who's that, I simply thought when I first saw her. Who's that?

Whatever she had planned, the pilot got us moved up quickly to first class, where the nuptials took place. Quite exquisite, in Eleanor's life there being no exception. But herself. Everything means something when you think about it. And if it weren't for Eleanor getting me into this, I would still be quite innocent. In fact, I'd not be here; but listen—there is a fine line which guides human behavior. Within five minutes, Eleanor, the pilot, and I were going at it in the cockpit.

[111]

It is an ongoing process. I cannot often recall the exact details of Eleanor's accomplishments. I am put in mind of where it was I was going to get to next. Who's that, I know I thought when I first saw her. What she was in the world doing. Something in between. Human sexuality. And all the fine lines that run out of reach. It may be interesting for some to behold such variants. We must yield to these. **Q**

My father's sister was a psychoanalyst—a Freudian; a recorder of early trauma. She saw patients in her apartment and they waited for her in the living room, sitting where we sat when we visited. From the couch they looked at the oddly flattened picture of a walled city, and from the chairs backed stiffly against the opposite wall they saw a portrait of Anna as a young woman.

Then Anna herself would appear, short and bargelike in the doorway, and they'd follow her into the next room, which held the couch, her chair, and a desk. At the end of their time they left the inner room through a converted closet, which led directly out to the hall, a dozen paces from where they'd come in.

As a child I knew this, that Anna hid her patients from one another. So I knew that what she did was shameful.

When I was to go out with Anna, I lost things. My shoes and barrettes disappeared. I cried because I had to wear a dress, or because the snarls pulled when my mother brushed my hair.

Anna took me to museums or to the zoo, and I became aware, in her presence, of my behavior—not so much of how it would be interpreted, but of the fact of interpretation itself. I felt her there watching me.

In return I watched back. I was her only niece and I knew she favored my cousins Danny and Jay. Still, I knew it was important that I like her. She said she enjoyed having a girl to buy presents for. She bought me a rag doll I could strap on my feet and dance with; she bought me an embroidered Mexican blouse. She pinched my cheeks and asked, "How's my ootsa-pootsa-pootsa?" and she encased me in the smell of powder and perfume. I rubbed at my cheeks to make them feel like my own again, and until they did I hid from her in the bathroom.

We struck a balance, Anna and I. She wanted and I withheld. She wanted to be a second mother; she wanted to understand me. She talked to me in that voice adults save for children, and I answered her in sentence fragments. I wasn't sure I wanted anyone to understand me, but especially not her.

In case anything happened to my parents, she was to be my guardian.

"In case anything had happened to us" was the phrase my mother used, years later when she told me about the arrangement. I was sixteen and we were sitting at the supper table over a final cup of coffee, which I was just learning to drink. I'd added sugar and cream that night, and the sugar outlined the bitterness until I swallowed it like aspirin. My parents drank theirs black and throughout the meal, and this presented itself to me as a virtue.

What I wanted to ask was *Why Anna?* What about my aunt Nora, who at least had kids. Or Sylvie, my other aunt, who left me room to breathe. Why Anna?

I didn't need to ask, really. The answer was expertise. I drank my coffee, which I had to hold in my mouth for a minute before I could get my throat to accept it. I looked at the table and felt my lips pushing out into a pout.

"The fifties were a terrifying period," my mother said, answering the question that must have been on her mind. "Especially after the Rosenbergs were arrested. If it happened to them it could have happened to anybody. Any left-winger. It could as easily have been us. People were losing their jobs; people were turning their backs on everything they believed in."

"Paulie, you can't explain the fifties if you just breeze by the Rosenbergs like that," my father said.

"I already know about the fifties," I said.

"When the Rosenbergs were first arrested," he said, "their boys were shipped from one relative to another, and then for a while they were in a children's home. One never has the advantage of foresight and there was no way to tell what was going to happen, but in case the worse should come to the worst, we wanted to work out something more stable for you."

"How come you didn't tell me?"

"It was a terrifying period," my mother said again. "We tried not to let it affect you."

"It was difficult to find a middle ground," my father said, "between your need for security and the sense that we had to teach you some kind of caution."

Caution. The susceptibility of children to trauma was as accepted in our household as their susceptibility to chicken pox, so my sense of security took precedence. I had no idea that throughout the fifties my parents half expected the FBI, although if I had known I doubt I would have understood the threat that implied. It would have been exciting; in fact, it would have been an honor.

As it happened, the FBI didn't visit my parents. They went instead to my mother's mother, a gentle, late-Victorian lady. They asked about my parents. Did she know they subscribed to *The Daily Worker*? Did she know what meetings they attended? Did she know their friends? She'd been coached not to talk to them. My parents had told her, as they told me later, that there was nothing illegal or unpatriotic about that.

My grandmother told the agents they should be ashamed of themselves, worrying innocent people while gangsters walked around shooting one another. They were very polite, she said. Well-dressed young men. And well-spoken. And couldn't my parents—*I know you haven't done anything wrong, but there's the child to consider*—couldn't my parents be more careful?

This, too, I learned later.

At the time, what I received were hazy warnings: Don't talk to strangers; don't accept candy; don't get into cars; and don't answer questions. I wondered if these were rules for all children or only for me. They made no sense to me, but I don't remember being frightened.

My memory of the fifties is spotty, though. My father was broad-shouldered in his suit and slender without it. When my mother dressed up, she carried white cotton gloves, which I never saw her wear. She collected money for the Rosenberg Defense Fund and she stored it in a milk bottle in the linen closet. On the day the Rosenbergs were executed, I added three pennies. I remember it clearly. My parents had gone to the vigil in Union Square and the woman who stayed with me kept the radio on. When the news came that they were dead, I asked her to take the bottle down and I dropped the pennies in one by one. She replaced the bottle between two stacks of blue towels, and for the rest of the evening I smelled copper on my hands.

It was during the fifties that my mother ran for City Council on the American Labor Party ticket. This meant nothing to me except that I got to stand in a crowd and watch her speak from a sound truck. God, she was beautiful! She narrowed her eyes like a sailor keeping watch in a storm and her voice came to me doubled, first in her natural voice, pitched to carry past the crowd and into the bricks of the wall behind us, then in metallic words, pounding through the loudspeakers. I rode first on one voice and then on the other, then tried to decipher both at once. The wind drove her hair back. She leaned into the microphone, and the men and women around me tipped their heads to watch her as if they were pulled. When she climbed down the ladder, I wrapped myself around her.

I wanted to be like her.

And then there was Anna. As she asked about my life, it sounded pointless and average. She asked about my girl friends, as she called them, or my boy friends, as though the word "friends" wasn't good enough, they had to be sorted and tagged by sex.

"What kind of games do you play with your girl friends?" she asked.

"I don't know. Just games."

"Do you play counting games?"

I shrugged. "I suppose. That's what kids do, isn't it?"

My rudeness went unacknowledged, and I confused it with freedom. Anna became more distant, which we never mentioned. I was asked to go places with her less often. I saw her when she visited my parents and when we visited her, although it seems to me the visits became less frequent.

Even when I was older, though, there was no question of missing a family party. These were major events. Thanksgiving was at Nora's; Christmas was at our house. We celebrated Christmas. My father's parents had been militant atheists, and when they came to this country they abandoned the Jewish holidays for Christmas, which must have struck them as less religious. It was a national holiday, my father said. Like Thanksgiving.

Anna's parties alone bore no relation to the calendar. She invited us when it suited her. The adults pulled the chairs out to complete a circle at the coffee table. They drank Dry Sack, or Cherry Kijafa, or Kahlua, names I remember because with each new arrival Anna pushed the conversation back to whatever it was they were drinking. Around those embedded sounds I formed my picture of sophistication.

I drifted back and forth between the adults and my cousins, who played games which excluded me in the inner room, and on my way between the two rooms I stopped at the dresser that faced the front door and I eased the lid off the squat blue jar that always sat there, being careful not to let it clink.

This was where Anna kept candy—raspberry-shaped drops with a liquid center, flat candies with a colored flower that ran all the way through. Sometimes I eased the lid back on and took nothing. More often I reached in with two fingers and lifted one out by the twisted end of the wrapper, being careful so the cellophane would not crackle.

I hadn't been forbidden to take them, but I couldn't remember having been told they were there. So to ask permission would have meant I'd been snooping.

My cousins clanked the lid. They reached their hands in to

dig for the piece they wanted. No one objected, and it had absolutely no bearing on my approach.

It was at one of those parties that Anna told a story she'd heard: A woman in a mink coat walked into a delicatessen on the Lower East Side and pushed in front of several customers. She waved her hand at the man behind the counter and said, "Listen, I won't take a minute. All I want is a herring. No, you better make that two herrings. And will you hurry? My chauffeur's double-parked outside."

The man behind the counter didn't move.

"Listen," she said, "I came all the way down here for a herring, the least you can do is sell me one. What's the matter? You don't want to do business? Will you listen a minute? Do you hear that? That's cars. Outside. They're honking. My chauffeur's blocking traffic."

So the man behind the counter lifted a herring out of the barrel and he held it out on a level with his face. And he looked at the fish and he looked at the woman. And he looked at the fish again and he looked at her again. Then he shook his head and he said, "Lady. It doesn't want to go with you."

The story stayed with me. That anyone in my family would be Jewish enough to tell it surprised me. So I remember the adults eating fish at those parties: pickled herring dripping its juice as they lifted it onto crackers; bright pink lox that left the smell of low tide on my fingers. And I think of Anna, almost square in her fur coat and fur hat, the way I remember her when she still took me out for afternoons, although I must have gone out with her in the summer, too, when she wouldn't have worn a coat. We walked down Seventy-fifth Street to Second Avenue, past the kids I played with, and the fur coat marked us, at least in my mind, even more than the fact that I lived in the only elevator building on a block of five-story walk-ups.

Neither the coat nor anything else embarrassed Anna. In front of the kids on the block; in front of the black woman who cleaned her apartment, whom she called Alice and who called her Miss Singer; in front of the waitresses in the restaurants she took me to and the elevator man in her building, she was at ease. Commanding. Like gravity itself. In tow beside her, I felt glaringly white and more than ever like one of New York's middle-class brats.

But even without Anna I knew what I was, and I knew that it kept me apart. The kids on the block said, "Borrow me the ball." I said, "Lend me." When I wanted to sound tough, I said, "Loan me." I had a carriage I could push my dolls in. I had books. When the ice-cream truck stopped on our street and I shouted up from the sidewalk, I could count on my mother dropping coins down, folded in a piece of white paper.

The other kids from my building didn't play on the street. I was the only one. I remember the first time a girl named Sharon came upstairs to play with me. She wanted to ride the elevator. I pushed the button for the second floor. Then we hung out the window in my room and she called down to the kids on the street, "Hey! Look where I am."

I knew exactly what my role was.

So when my mother relayed stories to me about my father's childhood and therefore also, of course, about Anna's, I hung on them.

I knew they'd grown up in a cold-water walk-up with the toilet in the hall—five kids and two adults in three rooms. I knew that my grandfather had taught Hebrew in the old country and that he was an educated man. I knew that in this country he lost job after job, and I knew that once a week my grandmother had boiled the wash on the stove and that the steam had packed the rooms until it squeezed out the air.

I went over and over these fragments. They formed a picture, but it wasn't one I could put my relatives into. Not the real people—not Anna, not my father. I accepted the stories, but I accepted them as mythology. The world had been strange before I was born and nothing I could do would make it solidify. As far back as I could trace the people I knew, they never matched up with the people my mother said they'd been.

I was in my late twenties and Anna was well into her seventies before it occurred to me to ask her about herself. We were at a family party and she answered me briefly, dismissing the question.

Then, a few days after the party, she asked me to have lunch with her at Schrafft's. We hadn't been alone together since I was a child and I watched, fascinated, as she settled her fur coat and hat into a mound on the chair between us. The waitress came and went. I drank my ice-cream soda with real concentration and I resisted the urge to pet her hat. We talked awkwardly about food, about wine, about things.

"You asked me the other day why I entered analysis," she said finally, "and I didn't answer you adequately."

I couldn't remember having asked her anything that intimate and I drew designs on the side of my glass.

"I had ended a love relationship and I hadn't been able to come out of it properly. So I began seeing an analyst."

I erased the designs and held my fingertip flat for the moisture to gather around it. As far as I could remember our conversation, what I'd asked her was nothing more than how she decided to become an analyst, although in the language of the time I may have said, literally, "How'd you get into analysis?" So I asked again what I'd meant to ask, and she said analysis was new at the time. It was in the air everywhere. It was tremendously exciting. She talked about the fascination of studying the human psyche in its endless complexity. I settled into the half-trance in which I generally listened to Anna, and we were on familiar ground again.

The next time I saw Anna, we were no closer for having talked. She was concerned that the woman who cleaned for her was stealing tablecloths, and I had fallen in love, first with a woman named Lucy and then, to make up for lost time, with women in general.

When, about a year later, Denise and I moved in together,

I introduced her into the family. She took a liking to Anna, and at parties she asked about the evolution of psychoanalysis and about Vienna in the twenties. She didn't mention the vaginal orgasm or Freud's famous faux pas, *What do women want,* and I'd mellowed enough to be grateful.

I was thirty-five when Anna died. My parents called with the news, and when I put down the phone, to my own surprise, I cried. There followed several weeks of slow, continuous eating, which I recognized about halfway through as a form of mourning.

My aunts took the job of sifting Anna's apartment and they asked me to choose something to remember her by. We walked a path through the boxes into which her dresser and closets had been emptied. I chose the jar she'd kept candy in. Then we sat in the dismantled living room and I asked about the affair Anna hadn't come out of properly.

"There was no one man that I know of," Sylvie said.

Sylvie is the oldest now, with Anna gone. She was very much the bohemian in her day and even now wears long scarves around her throat. She's a thin-boned woman, and like Anna, she never married.

"What about that one?" Nora said. "With the hair." She ran a hand from her hairline down over her forehead to indicate the way his hair fell.

"Red hair? Thin little eyebrows?"

"No no. Dark hair. Black hair. Fell forward like a bush."

Sylvie shook her head. "I don't remember that there was anyone in particular. Anna always had someone."

"*Ach,*" Nora said. "You never paid attention."

Nora is the youngest of my father's family, the only one of the sisters to have had children. She is heavy, but not the way Anna was heavy. She carries it softly.

"Who was he?" I asked. "When was this?"

"She used to bring him home on weekends, for dinner. He gave me chocolates wrapped in foil. If I was eight or ten, Anna would have been—what? Twenty-three? Twenty-five? He had a beautiful laugh. I remember that. And he and Father could go on at each other for hours."

"What did they talk about?"

"At that age, who listened? Sylvie, what did they talk about?"

"How would I know? I don't remember him. Religion, maybe. Palestine. Socialism. What Father always came around to."

"The theater," Nora said. "Father loved the Yiddish theater."

"I don't remember that he ever cared for the theater."

"And you don't remember the one with the hair? Such beautiful hair. God, I was half in love with him myself."

"You see?" Sylvie turned to me. "It's not Anna's affair we're talking about here, it's Nora's."

"Whatever happened to him?"

"He stopped coming with her."

"She never said why?"

Nora shook her head and I shrugged. Of course Anna never said why. If there had been anything to say. Maybe it was someone else—the guy with the red hair, or someone none of them had met. Some married man with three kids and a balding skull. A Hasid. A stockbroker. It was all beyond imagination. I couldn't picture Anna in love. Nora, yes; even Sylvie. But not Anna.

So this is what I know of Anna. Or this is what I don't know of Anna. I'm not sure which tells me more.

I know that Anna went to Vienna to study psychoanalysis. How she financed the trip I don't know. I know that, before she went, there was a love relationship which she failed to come out of properly; and I know I never asked what that meant.

As I get older, I think more about the lives my father's family lived before I was born. The lives they live apart from me. They say very little about themselves and it works at me like a hunger.

I'm slow to pick up on things sometimes. Only recently it hit me that the apartment where Denise and I live is laid out like the one in which they grew up—a railroad flat with the bathtub in the kitchen. We have five fewer people and much of the time we have hot water, but still it's small and it's awkward, with grates on the windows and roaches in the kitchen. Both of us work, and we talk sometimes about moving. I'm not sure whether it's to deny the family that fought its way out of an apartment like this or to keep faith with them, but I'm reluctant to leave.

Denise tells me I should buy a tape recorder and interview the family. She reminds me that they're aging, that what Anna might have said is already lost. I tell her that she's right, and I do nothing. I'm a respecter of silence, I've come to realize, collecting what stories are given, marking the gaps, assembling and reassembling them as if they would make a whole.

And so I own a blue jar in which I keep nothing—because candy makes my teeth ache; because nothing I can think of lives up to my idea of what it should contain; and because the candy I used to pick out of that jar never tasted as good in my mouth as it did while I was lifting the lid off, keeping it centered so it wouldn't clink. **Q**

Gene Fahey was a little, square-faced bulldog of the Faith and Father Spillone's right-hand man in the parish. He made his living selling furnaces or air conditioners, depending on the season, and, in his spare time, helped out around the church. On Sundays he stayed for all four Masses, doing the readings, taking up the collections, even filling in as an altar boy if one of the regular guys was sick. But his main mission was to the Catholic teenagers in town, especially the boys. His door was always open if we needed to talk, he said. It was his real job.

We were on retreat. We were sitting around in the main lodge at Camp Diamond. In the kitchen we had hung up a red-and-white-checked oilcloth for Father Spillone to sit behind. It was flopped over a rope strung between a stainless-steel sink and a cabinet full of big, shiny cans. You had to kneel on the floor, which was cement.

"Who's first?" Mr. Fahey asked. He had a loud, boomy voice full of enthusiasm. None of the other guys moved, so I said I would go. I knew he wanted me to.

I was shy when I got in the kitchen. I was used to the confessional at St. Brigid's, with its dark, carved wood and velvet kneeler and its curtain that you pulled to shut yourself in. You knew it was time to start when Father's panel behind the screen slid open and clicked, and you could hear his fat man's breathing.

"Go ahead," said the voice.

"Bless me, Father, for I have sinned," I said.

The red-and-white tablecloth was distracting right in front of my face. I thought of an Italian restaurant and pushed the thought out of my mind. I concentrated on my examination of conscience, then confessed anger, fights, making fun of people, cursing, taking the Lord's name in vain. I was staring at a drain set in a depression in the cement, imagining dirty mop water swirling down, the sucking sound.

"Is that all?" asked the voice.

"No," I said. "I was impure with myself fifteen times, impure with another five times. I had a lot of impure thoughts."

"I see," said the voice. "And how old are you now?"

"Sixteen and a half."

"A very dangerous age. These sins of impurity are especially dangerous. You must learn to control them before they become adult habits of sin. Do you understand?"

"Yes, Father."

"These sins with another. Were they with a girl?"

"Of *course,* Father!" I was shocked.

"Did they involve—touching?"

"Yes, Father."

"But no more than that?"

"No, Father."

"I see. That's a relief. And was this one of our Catholic girls?"

"No, Father. She's Jewish."

"Well." The voice made a long, whistling sigh. "That's another problem."

But he didn't pursue it. He gave me a stiff penance and told me to meditate on Our Lady's purity during the Hail Marys. Then he told me to make a good Act of Confession.

I sprinted into it.

"O my God, I am heartily sorry for having offended Thee."

The voice galloped along in Latin.

"Go and sin no more," said the voice.

Back in the big room Mr. Fahey was holding forth on faith in foxholes for a couple of the guys who expected to go in the service instead of to college. Mr. Fahey was a World War II vet so he knew a lot about war. He told them that we had to stop the Commies there in Vietnam or we'd just have to stop them later—in Japan or the Philippines.

"Penance in there, Mike," he said, pointing first at me and then at the door of a coatroom in which we had set up a kneeler. "Who's next? How 'bout you, Reidy?"

The guy he was talking to was a hood from Devon High. None of us had met him before the retreat, but he was supposed to be a wild kid. He had dropped a 409 into his '62 Chevy, and it went. He had a D.A. and carried a skinny comb in his shirt pocket to slick back the sides, which were shiny black slabs, and to tease the front, which jiggled like Paul Anka's. He straddled his chair backward and looked as if he'd just woke up, except it was nighttime.

"Chop chop," said Mr. Fahey.

Reidy rolled his eyes and unwound his legs and arms from the chair. He walked really slowly toward the kitchen, doing the stroll. Mr. Fahey stared at his back as if he knew he had his work cut out.

Later we were sitting around on old ratty couches and easy chairs in the room where the camp counselors hung out in the summer. There was a beat-up Coke machine, turned off, and two or three standing ashtrays, but we weren't allowed to smoke.

Mr. Fahey hustled in, rubbing his hands together as if he were freezing.

"Okay," he said. "The name of this retreat is 'A Catholic Young Man's Guide to Life and Love,' but really it's about sex!"

A couple of the guys giggled. Pat McGrath, the redhead, blushed so hard his freckles disappeared.

"First of all, we're going to review the facts," he said. "I know you guys think you know it all, but maybe you don't. I didn't at your age."

He unrolled some medical teaching charts that showed the female organs and pinned them to the wall. Mr. Fahey talked about ovulation and slid his finger along one of the tubes to show how the eggs come down.

"The uterus is also called the womb," he said. "You know in the Hail Mary where it says, 'Blessed is the fruit of Thy womb'?—well, this is it."

Someone sputtered, trying to hold it in.

"No cracks or I'll murder you," he warned.

He told how, if the egg wasn't fertilized, it came out every month with the menstrual blood. "That's when a girl has her period," he explained.

"On the ra-ag," Reidy whispered, really loud.

Mr. Fahey snapped around as if he'd been goosed.

"Mr. Reidy, I doubt you're such an expert," he said. He was pissed. "Maybe you'd like to share your superior knowledge with the rest of us."

Reidy's face kind of darkened, but I wouldn't call it blushing. He closed his eyes halfway as if he was really bored and jiggled his pack of cigarettes up and down in the other pocket from the one which held the comb. I think he wanted to smoke bad.

Mr. Fahey started talking about the vagina, which was pretty amazing to see up there on the wall. There were lines which led to neatly printed labels—VULVA, LABIA MINORA, LABIA MAJORA, CLITORIS. There was no picture of the clitoris, but he called it the "seat of female pleasure." There were also scrunched-up pictures, like belly buttons, labeled URETHRA and ANUS, but he didn't talk about those.

He went back to the other chart to show how the sperm goes up the vagina to meet the egg in the uterus.

"Presto! Conception!" he said. "Any questions?"

No one had any.

"I guess you all know what a penis is and what happens when it gets excited," he said.

That got a laugh. Even Mr. Fahey joined in. Beside me, Reidy made a wicked lip fart, but it was drowned out by the laughter.

"This is where we come in," said Mr. Fahey. "No pun intended."

More laughter. He grinned along for a second. Then his face got serious to let us know the jokes were over.

"As men, we have the God-given power, through the sex act, to create life," he told us. "The first thing we have to realize is: sexual intercourse for the purpose of procreation within the blessed sacrament of marriage is a beautiful and sacred thing."

"Aa-men," rasped Reidy.

Mr. Fahey stiffened but didn't react. He started talking about his own marriage. He and his wife had seven kids, but they still loved the sex act, he said. It was for reproduction, but it was also an expression of their love.

"Of course, you can do it in the normal way," he said. "But there're other things you can do."

"Like what?" Reidy asked, loud and clear.

Mr. Fahey glared at him for a long time.

"Well," he finally said, "since Mr. Reidy is so immature, I'll have to leave it to your imagination."

Reidy snorted softly at the ceiling. His mouth hung open. His eyes were closed.

"But the important thing," Mr. Fahey went on, "is that we always finish in the normal way."

"What about the rhythm method?" asked Tommy Scalpello, who wanted to be a priest.

"I'm glad you asked that, Tom," said Mr. Fahey. "The rhythm method is acceptable to the Church because it is a natural, not artificial, attempt to avoid conception. But if conception should occur, we accept it as the will of God."

Pat McGrath raised his hand and said he didn't understand the rhythm method. Mr. Fahey went back to the charts to explain the female fertility cycle. Then he told us he didn't want to spend any more time on birth control.

"If you guys need birth control, you're in big trouble," he said. "Mortal-sin trouble."

"What about rubbers?" Reidy asked suddenly. He sat up straight, eyes wide open.

"The Church rejects their use as artificial birth control," Mr. Fahey said.

"Too bad," said Reidy. He chuckled and settled back in his chair.

"The Church regards premarital sex, with or without birth control, as a grievous matter, Mr. Reidy," Mr. Fahey continued. "Are you married?"

"Not that I know of," Reidy said to the ceiling.

"In that case, I would listen closely," Mr. Fahey said. "And I would keep my mouth shut."

"I'll consider it," Reidy said. He folded his hands on his stomach and yawned.

There was a long silence while Mr. Fahey ran his palms, one at a time, back over his brush-cut hair. No matter how many times he plastered it down, it kept springing back. He was letting his temper cool.

"Okay," he said finally. "With the possible exception of Mr. Reidy, I suspect you fellows are confused about sex—what's right, what's wrong, how can you have fun with girls without endangering your immortal soul. Well, let's talk about it. Who wants to start?"

No one did. We were all looking at the linoleum floor. Except Reidy. From the sound of his breathing, he was really going to sleep.

"Okay," proposed Mr. Fahey. "Suppose you wake up from a dream and you're—aroused. Is that a sin?"

"No," I said.

"Very good, Mike," he said. "Why not?"

I shrugged as if I wasn't sure.

"Because there was no intention to sin," Mr. Fahey answered himself. "You didn't *decide* to have a sexy dream. But," he went on. "Suppose you do something to *prolong* the arousal? Or to *heighten* it?"

"It's a sin then," said Tommy Scalpello.

At that point McGrath cracked up. He put his fist in his mouth to stifle the laughter, but it leaked out in snorts and high-pitched shrieks. He turned the color of a fresh brick, and it deepened, as though the brick had gotten wet.

I could see Reidy's hand behind his chair, moving up and down in a blur. He was panting with his tongue out, and his eyes were crossed.

"Oh, yes, yes," he whispered in a girly voice. "Oh, yes!"

I think Mr. Fahey would have really blown up then. I think he might have punched the kid. But before he could do anything, Father Spillone walked in.

Father was normal in height and weighed about three hundred pounds. Mr. Fahey said it was glands. He said Father had once been a football star. He also defended him from people who didn't like the way he cleaned the chalice after Communion, which was to suck the wine off his thick fingers with smacking noises you could hear all over the church.

We all stood up except Reidy, who was pretending to be asleep.

"Did I miss the part about petting?" Father asked, as a joke. Mr. Fahey laughed in short barks. A couple of guys chipped in giggles. We sat down.

"I'm sure Mr. Fahey will cover what you need to know," Father said. "I just wanted to add that we're proud of you boys. You've got a tough assignment out there. We know it. You're the soldiers of Christ, and it's a tough daily battle. The enemy is all around, always there. And that's where your discipline comes in. An army can't win without discipline."

He paused so we could think about our discipline.

"Fellas, we know it's not easy," he went on. "Sometimes the other kids might make fun of you. Sometimes they might call you squares or sissies. But they really respect you, let me tell you. And you're never alone either, don't forget. When you say no to temptation, Almighty God knows. You're a hero to Him . . . And now, let us pray."

As one, we touched our foreheads, solar plexus, left and right shoulders, and folded our hands.

"Our Father, who art in Heaven . . ." we prayed. All except Reidy. He was sitting up again, staring around at the bowed, murmuring heads.

I guess he was really an atheist.

After the prayer, we took a break.

"Smoke 'em if you got 'em," Mr. Fahey shouted, fishing in his sport coat for his own pack. That was a big deal.

I didn't smoke yet, but I wanted some fresh air. It was late March, getting warmer. In the pine woods around the camp there were still piles of snow, pale smears in the darkness. They gave off a chill. Some peepers were tuning up in a nearby pond or creek. Pretty soon they would be twanging away.

Mr. Fahey called me over. He was smoking like a fiend, dragging deep and puffing out big clouds.

"That's a bad apple," he said, pointing to the parking lot, where Reidy had gone to stand by his car. "He's on the fast road to trouble."

I guess I nodded.

"I want you to help me out, Mike," he said. "The other guys respect you. If you joined in more, kind of tried to get the discussion going, they wouldn't pay any attention to that clown."

He turned to face me. "Or maybe you should just tell him to shut his dirty mouth. It'd mean more coming from you than from me."

"Maybe," I said.

I hung around the lodge a little longer, then walked out to the parking lot. Reidy was lounging against his Chevy, smoking.

"The hell with that asshole," he said.

He tossed his lit cigarette into the woods. It did little flips in an arc, like a goofy orange comet. He got in his car.

"The hell with my old man, too," he said. "Hey, Mike, you want to go for a ride?"

I decided right away. I didn't think about it. The guy made me nervous, but I wanted to. It was like when Sarah let me touch her. I just wanted to.

I got in the car.

Reidy fired it up. The engine roar was like a bomb going off. A thick blast of blue exhaust puffed past the rear window. He floored it till it wailed, then popped the clutch. We burned across the parking lot, chirped into second, and slid sideways, four tires smoking, onto the road. The inside of the car smelled like a rubber factory.

"Where to?" Reidy yelled.

I looked across the parking lot at the brightly lit lodge and the silhouettes frozen on the porch. They suddenly struck me funny, and I started to laugh.

"Take the—fast—road—to—trouble!" I yelled back, laughing crazily.

Reidy stomped on the gas pedal and, arching up from his seat, howled like a maniac.

The car shot away, roaring. **Q**

Writing under the title "The Little Magazines That Could," James Atlas briefed the readers of *Vanity Fair* about some 1986–87 newcomers to the literary fashion parade. Profiling new journals that were "preening themselves for a launch," he noted, by way of introduction, that even in this largely invisible (at least to the readers of *Vanity Fair*) world some had a reputation, and he cited *Grand Street* and *The Hudson Review* as reputable examples of the genre.

Normal and *Boulevard* aspire to gain a "reputation" and, depending on their skill, derring-do, and finances, may achieve the lofty state of a *Grand Street, The Hudson Review, The Paris Review, Antaeus,* or even the *Antioch Review.* Atlas neglected to say just what their reputations were based on other than to assert that they were held. With *The Hudson Review*'s reputation I have little quarrel. Its intelligence, its patient probing of our literary and social culture, and its sharp eye have won it a place on my regular reading list. *Grand Street* is another matter, and its "reputation" poses important questions about the current literary scene. With the Summer 1986 issue it closed out five years of publication. To their credit they did not issue an anniversary volume celebrating the event. But they might have.

As a bunch, literary magazines are a celebratory lot. Hardly a year goes by without some magazine issuing an anniversary volume, a retrospective review, a shout to the world that they have survived. Last year there seemed to have been more than usual of these self-congratulatory volumes, with every week bringing another extravaganza heralding the past ten, twenty, forty, fifty years of publication.

Partisan Review produced a golden anniversary book wherein William Phillips asserted that they were still opposed to "political reflexes, cultural cant, and literary obfuscation."

So are we all. The *PR* volume asked for something original from the old hands who have been the mainstays of the journal, and the likes of Nathan Glazer, Daniel Bell, and Diana Trilling all responded. George Stade closed the issue with a wonderful essay, "Confessions of a Political Imbecile," that was very un-*Partisan Review*-like. For some odd reason, *Shenandoah* (from Washington and Lee University) celebrated its first thirty-five years. I have been to lots of parties, but I can't ever remember anyone making a special case for toasting three tens plus five. There was a good deal to toast, since *Shenandoah* is one of those Southern literary magazines that just rolls along, publishing well-wrought stories, personal essays that remember what should be remembered (the death of Jean Stafford, for example), and accomplished poetry. Reynolds Price and Peter Taylor typify the *Shenandoah* approach: romantic, elegiac, stylized, civilized.

Looking at *TriQuarterly*'s twentieth-anniversary number (668 pages), one can see how obsessed the editors (from Charles Newman to Reginald Gibbons) have been with "contemporary" prose and the visual arts. Their concern with modernism and the "new" will soon produce another large volume of essays from the past twenty years. Bankrolling many of these literary efforts over the past twenty years has been the National Endowment for the Arts, and they have gotten into the celebratory act with *Buying Time,* an anthology of works by writers funded by the Literature Program. It is a *Who's Who* of literary culture, beginning with John Ashbery and ending with Charles Wright. They have a right to toot a horn, particularly in a year when some congressmen have discovered that literature can sometimes be "pornographic" and have been badgering the agency.

What does all this celebrating add up to? On the one hand, it is just self-promotion—the kind spoofed marvelously by Louis Rubin, Jr., and William Harmon in their parody, *Uneeda Review,* with its motto, "Like a Hole in the Head," and its special "23½ Anniversary Issue." There is also a feeling that such celebratory volumes are a way of making people take notice, of asserting a distinguished history, of laughing and crying at the same time. It is reminiscent of the individual who listed hobbies on a *vitae* as "Chess, strangling small animals and masturbation."

I think that more is at stake. *The Yale Review* celebrated a seventy-fifth anniversary, *Southern Review* just completed a half century, and *The Nation* had a party for its one hundred twentieth year. More than survival is being declaimed—it's our cultural history. At the *Antioch Review* (where I am, I confess, the editor), we are preparing for our fiftieth—due in 1991— with bumper stickers, tote bags, and T-shirts already on order.

All this leads me back to *Grand Street,* its reputation, and the current state of literary magazines. As every editor knows, they come in every shape and size known to mankind. There are oldies *(Kenyon, Sewanee, Hudson),* experimentals *(Fiction International, The Mississippi Review),* regionals *(Prairie Schooner, The Massachusetts Review),* and newcomers each year like *Grand Street* and *Raritan* vying for attention. New magazines appear because there is a gap in the market, because something has to be said, because there is loose change around, or because there is an ego on the roam. *Normal* is an art magazine responding to these glitzy times of ours; *Boulevard* just wants to be heard. Only time will tell about this particular set of newcomers; but the verdict—from *Newsweek* to James Atlas—appears in on *Grand Street:* it's a winner. But should we celebrate its reputation and recognize its goatlike stamina, its ability to forage in the literary wilderness, its having arrived at the top of the heap in just a short five years? I think not.

Its reputation has not been earned but by and large bought. And here I am talking about not just its ability to pay its writers handsome fees (a thousand dollars for a fiction piece, for example) but its misplaced notion that, for the most part, only the arrived, the already established, the sure chance can find a place in its pages. *Grand Street* risks almost nothing! What difference does *Grand Street* make except to those writers who are on the receiving end of its largesse? Has it broken new ground, found any new talent, excited the literate reader? To be honest, *No!* almost entirely on all counts. It publishes only the work of a handful of arrived American, Canadian, and British writers and critics.

Is *Grand Street* principally merely a halfway house for the commercial publishers, a prepublication outlet, a first-rights syndicate that accepts articles only in galleys? To have achieved a reputation on the basis of publishing Alice Munro, Ted Hughes, Penelope Gilliatt, Glenway Wescott, and Northrop Frye in the premier issue, and then following it up with Alice Adams, Hans Magnus Enzensberger, and Christopher Hitchens does not suggest an adventuring editorial view. Each issue is like a visit to the Saatchi art collection in London: for the most part an exploration of commercial rather than aesthetic values.

What does the success of *Grand Street* say to other literary magazines—particularly to the newcomers which are starting up outside New York and which struggle to gain some attention? The message is clear: Publish only the names, forget about the art of discovery, forget about the slush—play it safe. The question then becomes: What does a literary magazine stand for, what does it mean to have a "reputation"? I think it means that you have not only to publish "the best words in the best order," but also to enlarge the literary enterprise by engaging in the art of discovery.

There are some magazines that do try. *The Georgia Review* has arrived under Stanley Lindberg's editorship; *The Threepenny Review* under Wendy Lesser is a fresh voice on the West Coast; and *Raritan,* despite its *New York Review of Books* clone quality, has begun to pick up steam with fresh topics and writing. Its Spring 1986 issue had a fine piece on boxing by Ronald Levao; on dogs, horses, and traces of speech by Vicki Hearne; and one by Adam Phillips on composure. *Fiction International* regularly publishes exciting writers, many of whom have several books to their credit and who work seriously with too little exposure. *Open Places,* in Columbia, Missouri, has done some fine topical volumes that deserve notice.

Grand Street, on the other hand, features only two categories of writers: those who have just arrived (by arrived I mean a well-reviewed book in *The New York Times*) and those who have been around for so long that they have a "recognition" factor. Ironically, even *The New Yorker* (our most celebrated magazine) features, on occasion, new voices. The Summer 1986 issue of *Grand Street,* in contrast, featured William Gass, two fragments from Elinor Langer's soon-to-be-published autobiography, a Christopher Ricks piece on Thomas Beddoes (the first section appeared in 1982), and a potpourri of fiction and poetry by established figures. Despite its stylish cover and bold look, *Grand Street* is a timid and formless magazine. Its only aesthetic is an imitative one that chases after success by buying up stars—the Steinbrenner method.

Even *The New Criterion* (with its unabashed neoconservative aesthetic and nasty style) has shown promise. There is often a genuine effort to face important cultural and literary questions despite its penchant (reminiscent of the sixties *Ramparts*) for personalizing every issue. Hilton Kramer's commitment to the arts is without question, but the editors at *Grand Street* need *The New York Times* and *The Guardian* to tell them which way the wind is blowing. *Grand Street* should—on occasion—look beyond the banks of the Thames and the Hudson (lovely as they are). There are powerful currents elsewhere. Editing a magazine is like navigating a boat on a river: at times easy, at times dangerous, at times exciting. These are exciting times in the literary world, and the presence of new magazines should give us all a thrill. There is more out there than *Grand Street* could ever imagine. **Q**

Orient Point, Long Island.

It is very pleasant here. There is an enclave of houses done in what is, strangely enough, a sort of Mississippi mode, with imitation antebellum stone columns. There is a bay with green marshes at the front, which turns into a canal on the side, which turns into a green lagoon with lily pads and swans, oddly enough, in the back.

There was once a hotel across the canal, and this enclave was the staff quarters, giving it its humble air perhaps.

The setting is very beautiful but seems strangely tame. It is not as wild as my memories of the sea. The ducks and their little children file across the garden, escorted by swans when they reach the lagoon. The sight brought tears to my eyes for its tender domesticity. I have grown so tenderhearted that I shed tears at the slightest provocation. Then I found out that the ducks sometimes get eaten by otters. "It's the law of the jungle," said Grace.

It goes without saying I was horrified.

Grace Fox (the owner of the enclave) comes walking down the garden path. She is married to Constant Fox, the heart-throb. He is currently absent, conducting travels in the world. His pending arrival is actually a source of endless controversy and speculation. At least on my part it is.

The others are leaving from Manhattan at three-thirty to get to Long Island by six—such plots, you think, such long afternoons in the Jazz Age. In this raging green—everything is green outside of my marvelous imitation antebellum stone portico—there will be a storm tonight.

Much tender domesticity among the members of the Mississippi enclave, due at the moment to the family of six next door and the young couples. The others have not yet arrived.

. . .

This afternoon a man who could stand to lose about sixty pounds or more, with a handlebar mustache, bald, about forty-five, was in a rubber boat on the bay, weighing it down, with a tiny four-year-old boy. The latter asked me if he could sit on my lap, when he came over that evening. Naturally, I assented.

"Guess what?" said Andrew, the four-year-old boy. "Harry Locke drools. He drools on everything."

Then he lapsed into a pensive silence.

"And guess what else?" He looked at me intently. "I know how to play checkers."

"Time for your geography lesson," I said, and got out my atlas of the world. If there is one thing that interests Andrew, it is Africa. He is interested in the famine. Also, he has girlie pictures all over his room, even though he is only four years old. And Harry Locke drools all over them.

"Where am I from, Andrew?" I said, using the Socratic method.

"Louisiana."

(Pronounced Looziana—where did he get that? I don't pronounce it that way—suddenly he's a drawling Southerner.)

"Very good. And where are the starving people, Andrew?"

"Florida?"

"No . . . Come on, you remember."

"Africa?" in his high-pitched child's query.

"Good, Andrew."

"I can jump like a rabbit," he confided offhandedly.

"Now, what did we study yesterday?"

"Maps."

"So what did we learn about?"

"The map."

"But what is the study of maps? Of different parts of the world?"

He and his little sister, who had drawn near, start jumping

up and down at this (for it is known to them how to jump like rabbits). *"Geography,"* they chant, in rhythm with their jumps, ecstatic. *"Geography,"* they chant in a litany, with shining eyes.

Mrs. Langguth came out with the baby. I gave the baby four silver doubloons from Mardi Gras. The baby analyzed each one individually, inside her mouth, and then studiously threw them away.

The children run unsteadily across the lawn.

Tonight we are going to play checkers.

Cedric, the unwanted guest, is lounging in a deck chair on the lawn. He is the frequent though unwelcome visitor from the house on the bay. No one likes the people in the house on the bay because they won't let you walk on their lawn. None of them associates with our party except for Cedric, who comes over every afternoon promptly at the cocktail hour and stays for what seems like an endless time. He is considered a discordant element.

Grace rides up and down the road in her white Cadillac.

Mrs. Langguth, the mother of six, next door, is sitting on the front porch smoking cigarettes, adding the dark glamour of vice to her otherwise upstanding household.

The red-and-white-striped lawn chairs sit in the moonlight by the raging bay.

The guests are arriving, across the lawn. The young men are coming to us from Friday evening after work in Manhattan—wearing suits and ties and sunglasses, carrying their briefcases, uproarious yet exhausted, drunk yet sober, etc. They came in on the train in the parlor car and are somewhat the worse for wear due to the drinks.

The ducks, not to mention the otters, have already filled my heart with tender sorrow. I think I have had one too many cocktails. The Langguths insisted on concocting Sazerac cocktails, in my honor—"All the way up from Looziana," etc. I sit on my imitation antebellum stone portico, transfixed by the ducks and swans.

"So you came all the way up from Looziana on the *Cotton Blossom,* eh?" says the overweight fellow with the handlebar mustache, winking lasciviously, as though there is something ribald about Louisiana.

"*Southern Crescent,*" I politely correct him. "The train."

"Yes, I took that train once. The *Orange Blossom,* heh heh. My heart belongs in Dixie."

I took a queasy excursion to town for a drink with the young couples. There is a very nice bar called Claudio's with ceiling fans and an old tile floor and green tablecloths, in a section of Orient which is known, oddly enough, as Port of Egypt.

John said he wanted to name his first child Thompson and his second Elektra. Why Elektra, I wonder. It is not like him. He is what you would call a normal, regular guy, and all of the couples are normal and regular, with double standards, the men in banking jobs, the women with artistic interests. The men are jocks, but with certain eccentricities, like Sam leaning over at dinner, pedantic in his black-rimmed glasses, to say, "When Jane and I have sex, it's incredible, it's unbelievable, it's like—" making some ecstatic, lurid description, readjusting his glasses, and simply continuing dinner.

They are the love couple. She is a good, strong, sweet-hearted, fine girl. She does not have much personality. She is stupefied—in a constant state of even slightly ashamed stupefaction—by the amount of sex she has with her husband. He is a fellow who is endowed with everything—wit, brains, personality—and to top it off, he is at the same time strong and tall and filled with sex ardor.

The amount of his sex ardor keeps his wife in a constant

state of stunned love-embarrassment. In a way, she is cowed. Although she is a very big-boned, very big, very tall girl, in his arms she is cowed.

Men, when they get together, find interesting the dullest subjects. How to get the ladder to the pier. Whether the water should boil longer. How much grease to use on a screw. How to repair the boat. Who should keep score in the bridge game.

Water-skiing, tennis, and the like, the occupations here; that people should concoct forms of amusement which they ply with such seriousness always strikes me as lovably absurd —the couples playing bridge at the card table on the lawn, the men wearing silly sports caps.

The bay is like a pleasure kingdom. The red-and-white-striped lawn chairs, the children in rubber boats far out into the bay, and people taking drinks on their front porches.

Everyone seems to be slowly getting plastered all afternoon.

The weeping-willow trees, some white wood deck chairs in the Langguths' garden. The rustling of the leaves, the waning light on the bay, and the green canal. The swans on the green lagoon. The drama of the twilight.

The love couple are having sex in the laundry room, where they retired after having embarrassed everyone in the kitchen, where the torrid scene began.

I brought the baby a small red wallet with a little chain that she could use as a purse. She promptly hung it on her nose, and dissolved into a fit of mirth.

Andrew, looking on, has a sweetness in his brow. He looks

at the baby with a tenderness beyond his years. It is the consideration for others that is his chief attribute, even though he is only four years old.

Andrew takes a great interest in my boyfriends, although his conception of them is confined to whether or not they have a mustache, and his conception of a mustache seems to take in a wide variety of attributes.

"Time for your geography lesson," I said to Andrew. "Where is Paris?"

Making an expression of polite interest, he studied the world atlas and put his little hand upon the page.

"California?"

"Now come on, Andrew, you remember. There are seven continents in the world, remember?"

"Guess what?" he said shyly. "There's a continent called Nuttin and they make nuts there."

"Oh really? Well, there's a certain continent I know of called Europe, with a certain country called France, and a certain person I know forgot the whole entire thing."

"Do you like cole slaw?" Andrew says urgently. "I don't."

Conversation with a four-year-old involves wide leaps among a disparate variety of subjects.

I spent a good deal of time with Andrew. We made a secret hiding place in a pole by the canal and put a marble in it. I put in three small tiles with the initials of the children. Andrew put a secret present in the secret hiding place that night, but it floated out to sea, as he dropped it in the bay.

We observed the swans. The swans were acting extremely peculiarly. They seemed to be in amorous stupors, taking their cue, perhaps, from the love couple. The swans flapped their wings heatedly and raced toward one another in the bay.

We built a sand castle and tried to dig a hole to China.

That night there were stars in abundance, including shooting stars.

I bought presents for the children. I would gladly buy them everything in sight.

At night I am consumed by worry for the children. Waves of worry consume me, on their behalf.

I couldn't sleep—is it the tender domesticity and the country, the bay, the gardens, the green marshes, and the slant of light? One's like a stranger in his rooms, his own rooms. But there is the black glamour of the night, the rustling of the leaves.

"Do you want to play the marvelous marble game?" said Andrew.

"No, thank you," said the moody bachelor.

"What's your philosophy?" said Andrew. (After temporarily despairing of geography, I have moved on to philosophy.)

"I haven't the foggiest," said the moody bachelor. "What do you mean, what's my philosophy?"

"Philosophy, philosophy," the children scream in tragic attitudes, although ecstatic at their newest realm of knowledge.

"Okay, okay, okay. I get the picture. But I don't have a philosophy."

"Do you like cole slaw?" asked Andrew. Whether or not a person likes cole slaw, also if he has a mustache, are Andrew's real gauges of character, and much more important to him, quite frankly, than either geography or philosophy.

As it happens, the moody bachelor does have a mustache, therefore automatically inciting Andrew's love. Andrew asked him why he had a mustache, but the moody bachelor made his standard reply, "I haven't the foggiest," which, I might add, is an answer that Andrew tends to find hilarious, if enigmatic.

"Let's play the Silent Game," said the moody bachelor. "Sometimes Big People need peace and quiet. Okay, buddy? Do you know how to play the Silent Game?"

"I haven't the foggiest," said Andrew, collapsing in hilarity.

The children are swimming in the bay with rubber boats. "Lower your voice, F.R.," their mother calls from the shore. F.R. always picks fights. The man with the handlebar mustache, who could stand to lose about seventy pounds, sits alone under a beach umbrella, pensive and a tad on the morose side.

The swans are on the green lagoon.

F.R. (son of the overweight fellow with the handlebar mustache and not so trim himself) comes trudging across the lawn, wrapped in a towel, carrying a toy pail. The forlornness of children is always enough to break your heart.

There is a floating bar in the bay—and a dinner party, with long tables in the twilight.

The drama of the twilight. **Q**

After a generation of radical pacifism, it is hard to find an audience that is not immune to the shock value of Joanna Macy's paradox (see it in her *Despair and Personal Power*) that vulnerability is power. It is startling to find Simone de Beauvoir saying in *The Second Sex* that "marriage is an obscene bourgeois institution" only if one does not know that she is repeating a long-established commonplace among French literary intellectuals. When David Gress, commenting in the April *New Criterion* on the repetitive nature of Michel Foucault's debunking spirit, says that after reading a few chapters of any one of Foucault's books "it is fatally easy to generate Foucaultian critiques of any institution, practice, or attitude one happens not to like," he is only saying what any nightclub habitué could say after listening to the first few minutes of a Lenny Bruce paradox-laced program or *Saturday Night Live*.

The paradox, of course, is a respected enough rhetorical device. As an organizer of information it is as useful as the metaphor, which is itself a reversal of received opinion—at least until as a dead metaphor it becomes part of received opinion. To George Bataille (see his commentary in the beautiful *Prehistoric Painting: Lascaux or the Birth of Art*) what defines the human being is the paradoxical spirit of transgression aroused by the discovery of the divine animality from which he has been separated. Bataille might have been closer to the truth if he had seen the human being defined not by this particular paradox but by the capacity to perceive paradox. This capacity is inseparable from the condition of self-awareness in an environment in which—because of the gaps between nature and nurture, appearance and reality, signifier and signified, diachronic and synchronic—conflicting perspectives are as possible as despair at not finding one master perspective. Paradox at its best is so consciousness-expanding and reality-revealing, and at the same time so exciting, that one of the easiest things to understand is the confusion of its effects with the effects of drugs and alcohol.

To see how enlightening paradox can be in these paradox-glutted times one need only read Peter Berger (*Partisan Review,* 4, 1985) on the relation between liberation and alienation, or Leszek Kolakowski (*Encounter,* March 1986) on the indispensability of a taboo system to communal life. Both of these essays argue, with a civility that assumes the right of other perspectives to exist, for a reversal of current pieties about individualism and irreverence. Both would be objectionable to that desecrating hyperindividualist Iago, for whom personal autonomy and a respect for taboos are utter incompatibles.

Iago's paradoxes, like Oscar Wilde's, are dogmatic. He would appreciate the latter's "Conscience and cowardice are really the same things"—though he might protest that he had already clearly implied it. The effect of Wilde's paradox depends greatly on a reader predisposed to confuse wisdom with entertainment and ethics with aesthetics, who would like to have settled once and for all the complex relation between interdictions of conscience and courageous individualism. The structural brilliance of Wilde's formulation, unlike Berger's paradox, tends to swallow up any possible rebuttal— especially the rebuttal that acts of conscience, given the extent to which Wilde's paradox has become a cultural commonplace, may have to be especially courageous. One suspects that the aim of Wilde's paradox is to subvert conscience, not clarify it, meanwhile protecting itself with the disclaimer that it is only entertainment for the more sophisticated sort of cabaret clientele. It anticipates, in fact, the closed and dogmatic paradoxes of the world of Big Brother in Orwell's *Nineteen Eighty-four:* WAR IS PEACE, FREEDOM IS SLAVERY, IGNORANCE IS STRENGTH. It anticipates, too, that combination of brilliance and perversity that in the late sixties and seventies made Roland Barthes so irresistible.

Iago's paradoxes are no less closed than Big Brother's.

When he sets it down to his victims that all that appears to be fair is really foul (echoing the three witches in *Macbeth*), he is offering them not a tentative perspective which, if considered judiciously, might refine their decisions but a liberating rule-of-thumb solution to the problem of appearance and reality. It is not odd that Othello, biased for rule-of-thumb decisions as he is, believes Iago to be a fellow who "knows all qualities, with a learned spirit,/Of human dealings." As a paradoxer Iago does not honor adversary positions unless by pretending to he can serve his own ends. Indeed, like a faith healer he implies that his own position is an absolute beyond all possible counter positions, they having been considered in depth and disposed of ahead of time. His view of the world, therefore, has the advantage of being superficially clearer than that of the playwright, whose own view is handicapped by the value it places on faith and imagination. This handicap, of course, has something to do with the fact that the playwright's view has outlasted Iago's. It may also have something to do with the fact that Raymond Aron is already showing signs of outlasting that brilliant paradoxer Jean-Paul Sartre.

Thanks to the playwright's "handicapped" view of reality, we are able to appreciate the paradox that in spite of his apparent sophistication Iago is really quite provincial in the way that cynics (to say nothing of faith healers) usually are. This is the provinciality that marks so much American humor, whether we see it in Mark Twain, Ring Lardner, and Kurt Vonnegut, for instance, or in our alehouse entertainers and small-town wiseguys, whose credibility depends on their ability to give the impression that they are inside dopesters with special access to the infinite corruption of the world. To put their function in terms of Shakespeare's play, they are able to censor out of consciousness the worst possible news: that if Desdemona is just as good as she appears to be, there is an unsettling mix of good and evil in the world that resists easy paradoxical reduction.

Iago's provinciality is an intense and energy-concentrating

kind of specialization, the short-term effectiveness of which is inseparable from severe distortions of consciousness. This kind of specialization was abundantly on display among the literary intellectuals at the early 1986 PEN conference in New York. Referring to the unmodulated apprehension of evil (especially American evil) expressed by writers like Günter Grass and Allen Ginsberg, the Israeli writer Amos Oz pointed out that "whoever ignores the existence of varying degrees of evil is bound to become a servant of evil." Raymond Aron made pretty much the same point thirty years ago in *The Opium of the Intellectuals,* which among many other things is a book about the provinciality of a class of people inclined to define itself as by nature immune to provinciality, convinced as it is that it has a monopoly on truth and reason and a commission to function as the conscience of humanity. When Aron speaks of Sartre's combination of ethical radicalism and ignorance of social structures, he might also be describing Iago, who anticipates the modernist and postmodernist hero's rejection of bourgeois morality and the social observances that structure it—with the difference, of course, that at heart Iago is not an ethical radical but a radical amoralist. So Iago—like the provincial that he is, paying no attention to the varying degrees of evil—says categorically to the bourgeois Roderigo that what he takes to be loving is really lusting, and what he takes to be Desdemona's "blessed condition" is only the fair outside of her essential sexual insatiability.

Henry James got a taste of this kind of provinciality in Paris in the mid-1870s, when he spent time with Flaubert and other literary intellectuals in the rue du Faubourg Saint-Honoré. Leon Edel writes that despite James's joy in the "wit and intellectual power of the Flaubertians, he found them also distinctly insular." In one of his dispatches to the *New York Tribune* he observed that

"French literature abounds in books in which particular tendencies have been pushed to lengths which only a sort of artistic conspiracy of many minds could have reached, but which seem like mere blind alleys of thought, where explorers perish for want of having taken heed of possible issues to right or left."

This anticipates Aron, to say nothing of Jean-François Revel, who is currently belaboring the ethical and political radicalism of the French left for its blind alleys of thought.

We can place some of the blame for this kind of provinciality on what Roger Shattuck in *The Innocent Eye* calls the Demon of Originality. No one is more likely to sound provincial than the person whose fear of not being accepted will not let him relax from the effort to sound original on all subjects in all circumstances, ideally by way of startling reversals of received opinion. Failure, with its side effect of demoralization and confusion, is the aim of the Demon of Originality's blackmailing mandate: Be first or be nothing. He must discourage attention to varying degrees of originality, just as the Demon of Perfection must discourage attention to varying degrees of evil. No doubt they are ultimately the same devil. If a society believes that the most important thing is to be first, much that is evil will pass for good, while the voice of the truly necessary innovator gets lost in the general hubbub of originality. In the meantime, for better or worse the world is speeded up, perhaps to the point of panic and totalitarian slowdown.

Iago, who is like the talented young man from the small town whose sharp eye for the main chance gets him quick success in the big city, clearly takes delight in his originality. "Divinity of hell!" he exclaims after his brilliant manipulations of Cassio and Othello in Act 2, Scene 3, "When devils will their blackest sins put on,/They do suggest at first with heavenly shows,/As I do now"—as if no mere mortal had ever done it before. In fact, his faith in his originality has a good deal to do with his ultimate failure: it keeps him from learning from the mistake of previous fanatic revengers no less convinced of their originality. The Demon of Originality, like his alter ego, the Demon of Perfection, does not encourage the reading of history.

But if Iago had been capable of that kind of learning he could not have become the powerful model that he is for the ethos that finds fulfillment not in a commitment to communal life that is at once law-abiding and magnanimously critical but in transgression. Many have been struck with the disproportion between what has been done to Iago and what he does in order to balance the books in his favor. In fact, Coleridge in a famous passage speaks of Iago's "motiveless malignity." In his splendid *Magic in the Web,* however, Robert B. Heilman points out that by "motiveless" Coleridge means that Iago's conduct "cannot adequately be accounted for by the commonplaces of cause and effect." Certainly the man who wrote *The Statesman's Manual* did not have to read the Marquis de Sade's *Philosophy in the Bedroom* or Bataille's interpretations of the Lascaux cave paintings to discover how far the motives of malignity could exceed the commonplaces of cause and effect. Indeed, Coleridge can help us see that with *Othello* Shakespeare was preparing us for the cultural paradox that we have been trying to live with for a long time now: that transgression as an end in itself can be a highly satisfactory kind of self-transcendence.

The stated cause of Iago's action is revenge because he has been passed over for promotion, but it is soon apparent that revenge is only the occasion for an existential assertion of his will against a society that is denying him (as any viable society would) an opportunity for an intransigent realization of his full potential for an original and autonomous life. Perhaps this is easier to see if we come at him by way of such transgressors as Nietzsche, the Dadaists, Gide, Artaud, Céline, Bataille, Sartre, and Genet. In the company of such talented and determined reversers of received opinion it is possible to see that there is something far beyond the commonplaces of revenge in Iago's willingness to put all in hazard as he goes about the business of inventing himself. Now it becomes apparent that he is the very mimic of the artist as he dares to take on even his own creator, functioning as author, producer, director, stage manager, and star of a counterplay.

That counterplay attempts to reveal the subversive truth about the creator of both play and counterplay: that he is, at least covertly, where all true artists should be, on the side of transgression, and that if he hadn't lost his nerve (as he had earlier lost it with Falstaff) the relation between play and counterplay might have been reversed, so that he would have broken out of the closet of bourgeois morality and been sainted for his authenticity three and a half centuries before Sartre put a halo on Jean Genet. Further evidence of such a paradoxical possibility can be found in Iago's last words after his counterplay collapses and he is left alone but undaunted and unrepentant on his bare stage: "Demand me nothing: what you know, you know:/From this time forth I never will speak word." Liberated from the bourgeois prison house of language and from the bad faith with which it conspires, he goes off into a silence that shouts both his and his creator's triumph.

One consequence of looking at the play from the counterplay's perspective is that you miss seeing that Iago is a terrorist —just as you miss seeing that a Shiite hijacker is a terrorist if you see him from his perspective, from the inside, in which case he probably becomes an utterly committed young idealist willing to put his body on the line in service to a self-transcending cause that brings him the bonus of excitement and peace of mind. From Iago's point of view, "terrorist" is the establishment's put-down term, its characteristic way of using language to mask its pusillanimous fear of striking out boldly for life, and he would recognize with ironic pleasure that the distance between the term as signifier and himself as signified is a measure of his liberation. Iago's case, of course, differs from that of the hijacker in that those who are subjected to his reign of terror think he is trying to help them: that in their confusion and agony they can trust him to bring them peace of mind by making the complex simple and the crooked straight. He can do this with a terrorist's undivided mind, however, because he truly believes that ethically, epistemologically, and ontologically things are just as simple as Wilde's paradox implies. Therefore, Othello with his pathological dependence on total peace of mind is an easy victim. The price of his peace of mind is absolute faith in Iago, the rock upon which his own terrorist act, the murder of Desdemona, is founded and transvalued into a jihad-like sacrifice to his violated honor.

Iago can on occasion appear to agree with Amos Oz that evil exists in varying degrees. For instance, after Cassio has caused the drunken uproar in Act 2, Scene 3, he counsels the outraged Othello that "men are men; the best sometimes forget," and shortly thereafter counsels the self-castigating Cassio to see the affair in a more rational perspective. But this is only a device; a terrorist who really believes Oz will quickly lose his occupation. Iago's liberating function is to relieve others (and no doubt himself) of the burden of having to distinguish among degrees of evil. To believe that evil exists in varying degrees implies not only the reality of a measuring good, also existing in degrees, but the moral obligation to pay close attention to the distinctions. It implies, too, a moral obligation not to relax from the effort to distinguish between transgressions aimed at serving civilization (as metaphor and paradox at their best do) and transgressions aimed at subverting it. It implies, in short, the moral obligation to do what the play does: oppose Iago.

In *The Climate of Violence,* Wallace Fowlie points out that Sartre, arguing for the canonization of Genet in *Saint Genet, Actor and Martyr,* "makes clear his conviction that evil is a myth created by the respectable members of society." This is not the sort of conviction that would give Oz comfort, but it does make Sartre sound like a terrorist-liberator whom Iago, up to a point, could agree with. Most likely, too, Iago would have found congenial company, again, up to a point, among those critics whom Jean Paulhan, former member of the French Academy, called terrorists because they were "intent on challenging creation at all times, dedicated to seeking the sublime within the loathsome, greatness within the subversive, demanding further that each work commit and compromise its author forever." Indeed, if Iago had read Paulhan's laudatory introduction to Pauline Reage's attempt at a paradoxical transvaluation of the pornographic in her *The Story of O*, he might have suspected that Paulhan, too, belonged in that company.

But the point beyond which Iago could not go with such terrorists is the point at which it becomes clear that their terrorism is not authentically self-serving but is aimed, however misguidedly or self-deceivingly, at extra-personal ends. Thus he could cheer on the Japanese dissidents and the German Baader terrorists, as Genet did, only so long as he was able to believe that they were in the business of terror for the same reason that he was—"for my peculiar end," as he tells Roderigo in the opening scene of the play. And those who, like Othello and Roderigo, naïvely identify their peculiar ends with self-transcending causes are easily manipulated into terrorism, or into offering safe haven to terrorists who claim, as various IRA killers have, that their violent acts were politically motivated. The honest Iago would be much more at home with those well-heeled transgressors who, as Nicholas Pileggi reports in *Wiseguy: Life in a Mafia Family,* would not enjoy dining out unless the dinner could be paid for with a stolen credit card. Such fellows "have some soul," as he tells Roderigo about the class of persons in which he himself belongs: they "do themselves homage."

In his poem "The Anatomy of the World," John Donne, Iago's great contemporary, writes, "The new philosophy puts all in doubt." One might, in fact, make a case for his affiliation with the Greek skeptics, Sextus Empiricus in particular, who had the effect on their contemporaries of reducing to the doubtful much that they had believed certain. But the skeptics also dealt in peace of mind—"mental tranquillity" is Sextus' term—and one remembers Othello as he experiences the agonizing consequences of attempting to prove love as he might prove the strength of a military adversary: "O, now, for ever/ Farewell the tranquil mind!" But Sextus believed that the tranquil mind was possible only if one could suspend judgment in the presence of fanatics and dogmatists who promise peace of mind only on the most categorial terms. Iago only pretends in the interest of his own power to stand by the skeptics' paradox that, contrary to common sense, mental tranquillity and uncertainty are compatibles, for instance, when in Act 3, Scene 3, he advises Othello to "leave it to time"—that is, not to jump to hasty conclusions about Desdemona's honesty. Behind this ploy, however, there is the deformation of consciousness and concentration of energy of the dogmatist or fanatic whose own mental tranquillity derives from the certainty that he can control time. He even has a good deal of the charisma that Max Weber believed to be so crucial to institution building— except that, like Paulhan's terrorists, his fanatic energy is directed against the institutions that threaten his transgressive autonomy.

Our own new philosophies have for some time now been calling all in doubt, and like Iago, but unlike the Greek skeptics, their hounding motivator is the Demon of Originality. Ostensibly, too, they deal in peace of mind with their promise to relieve us of the burden of discovering the significant relationship among text, author, and world by prescinding from the latter two—though, to be sure, they come to their transgressive chores reeking of the world and as authors in disguise quite as much as Iago is a playwright in disguise. One of their problems, however (it is Iago's as well), is that the Demon of Originality is covertly against peace of mind, since he can tolerate no resting place and must by all means keep his victims from learning what he knows so well: that innovation is always likely to be the preface to confusion, if not cliché, and therefore ultimately to a skepticism about the value of any innovation whatever. Perhaps it is the Demon speaking in a moment of rare candor whom we hear in Nietzsche's poem "Ecce Homo":

All I touch turns first to light,
Then to ashes black as night:
A flame is what I am indeed!

As they continue the assault of romantic individualism on what they take to be paralyzing custom, taboo, and convention, the new philosophers establish their connection with Iago rather than Sextus Empiricus—a hardworking physician trying to keep his feet on the ground in a world full of passionate certainties. Coming after Nietzsche's discovery that God is dead, our new philosophers, who, like Iago, are "nothing if not critical," have inherited the mantle of comfort bearers in an environment in which a proliferation of dogmatisms intensifies the threat of anomie and impotence. In such an epistemologically noisy environment it is not surprising that the new philosophers, convinced that not only God but the author, too, is dead, tend to come on with all the certainty of dogmatists —and sometimes even sound like Paulhan's terrorists. How parlous their situation is Eugene Goodheart makes clear in *The Skeptic Disposition:* "The incorrigible persistence of what the deconstructive critics call mystification and naïveté has its source in the inextinguishable human need for values and the assent to values that we call conviction." In terms of Shakespeare's play, this is the need to believe in Desdemona's honesty and to accept as corollaries all the interdictions that, by protecting her from egotistic transgressors, make her honesty possible.

The late seventeenth-century playwright and critic Thomas Rymer, who seems to have been protected from Donne's new philosophy by a dogmatic cast of mind, believed that *Othello* was a "bloody farce" with no instruction for the audience. Such an interpretation implies a peace of mind about potentially unsettling matters that we can only envy now. But paradoxically, it is an interpretation from Iago's perspective: a bloody farce is exactly what, in his view, he has brought off, and we can imagine his barely contained laughter as he goes wordlessly off stage, convinced that he has success-fully countered his creator's efforts to make a tragedy. He has conned Rymer just as effectively as he has conned Othello, Roderigo, and Cassio.

We may envy Rymer, too, because his dogmatic clarity about the play protects him from the high-risk situation the author has voluntarily put himself in. The latter has projected into the play his own and every man's potential for a vengeful and nihilistic attack on civilized order, and his own and every man's sense that it is this potential that makes civilization such a precarious enterprise. He dares to let Iago have all the weap-ons he needs to make a fair fight of it, even at the risk of appearing to be in collusion with him. He dares, one might say, to go with him to what the poet Browning calls "the dangerous edge of things," as Conrad in *Heart of Darkness* dares to go to the edge with Kurtz, in order to define more precisely where and what that edge is, perhaps even to cast light into some of the terra incognita beyond it where Iago had his genesis. And this dangerous journey dramatizes once more the para-dox, so offensive to the slaves of the Demon of Originality, of the interdependence of discipline and liberation, of struc-ture and meaning, not only in art but in the effort to make a civilization. **Q**

There's a train strike going on, but do I know it? Hell no, I don't speak French. Father wanted me to be a doctor so I speak German. Would have learned Latin, only Father feared that would make me a Catholic. So all I know is, a driver will meet me at Charles de Gaulle Airport and take me to Gare de Saint-Lazare somewhere inside Paris.

Young fellow with puppy-dog brown eyes, goopy hair, and sign with my name on it greets me outside Customs and Immigration, where they don't bother to stamp your passport anymore (this is the week *before* the bombings), and he doesn't speak English and I don't speak French so I mime getting to the train station, wishing the whole time he spoke English or at least had the decency to wear a chauffeur's cap. See, this was all arranged through a friend in Paris who is European editor of *Screen International*, which is the British version of *Hollywood Reporter*. She once worked for Darryl F. Zanuck and knows all about limos. She was to have picked me up at the airport herself and then gotten on board the train for Deauville with me, only she got an invitation to go to Leningrad.

While I'm mispronouncing *gare* eighteen different ways, goopy hair's nodding and saying, *"Oui, Deauville,"* not pronouncing the last three letters in order to confuse me further, and next thing I know we're no longer in Paris but on an open stretch of highway that looks like Bavaria. (Dad not only insisted I learn the goddamn language but sent me at sixteen to *school* in Germany, and now my point of reference vis-à-vis Europe is totally askew, though as a heavy monetary contributor to Simon Wiesenthal I've come to believe that Frenchmen are really nothing but Germans with chic accents.)

I am delivered right to the door of my hotel in Deauville, where fall's long shadows are cutting a rug across the flower-bed display in the driveway that spells out in posies "Royale."

That's the hotel. The Hôtel Royale smells like all four-star luxury hotels in France: perfume, soapy water, and canine urine. My room, 506, is on the fourth floor, very confusing, and the bathroom is larger than the bedroom, but, thinking back to school days, am exceptionally grateful it's not down the hall. Fill the bidet with ice, drop in bottle of champagne (old school trick), and walk about town to declare my presence.

The Deauville Film Festival's been going on for four days and already I've missed the two main events: when the Hôtel Royale named two of its suites after visiting celebrities. Last year it was Liz Taylor, who got food poisoning from the mayonnaise at the poolside buffet and gave every evidence of being in danger of throwing out her back if she were made to barf up her guts in her bathroom, which would be every bit as large as her bedroom.

This year the Hôtel Royale named suites for Tony Curtis, and Mike the Dog from *Down and Out in Beverly Hills.* This Mike's a real pig. Has his picture taken wherever he goes. Curtis is gone by the time I show up, and as I'm promenading about town during the lunch hour, I don't see a single soul except for some gendarmes with machine guns.

Lobsters are $100 apiece at Augusto, a nondescript seafood restaurant three long blocks from Royale. We take a cab. I am with Elaine Kaufman, who owns Elaine's, the restaurant in New York where Woody Allen eats but never talks, and four other people; in toto, three men, three women. Besides Elaine, there's an actress whose name I never get right and her tall agent, named Heather, and besides me, there's Jack, a playwright who sings "Ol' Man River" between courses, and Michael, a young fledgling stockbroker from Minneapolis whose sister is an American paparazza named Dakota. The women's menus do not list prices. I suggest we split a dessert and get out. Elaine orders six lobsters. "What do you want to start?" she asks the group. A bank loan. She orders a platter of periwinkles, crabs, clams, oysters.

Local drink is calvados, made from apples. It strips the enamel off your teeth and removes the need for brushing. Elaine and I go see our one movie, *The Glenn Miller Story*, because June Allyson is being saluted. Allyson is accompanied by her husband, David, a retired dentist who is now an actor. Her eyes still turn into slits when she smiles. The festival's Ruda Dauphin, who arranges these homages and wears silk dresses, says there are only two people left to be saluted: Ava Gardner and Cary Grant. Dauphin asks them every year. Every year they give her the same answer.

Miriam Wiesel, wife of Elie Wiesel, is told by the gendarmes that the reason they are carrying machine guns at the film festival is that they are protecting Americans and Jews. She says demurely, "Then I must thank you twice." They don't get it. James Coburn holds a press conference and says Charles Bronson hates Mexicans.

After *Glenn Miller*, Dauphin grabs me because Jean Negulesco is being decorated by François Leotard, new minister of culture, who wears Italian suits. He's an improvement over Jack Lang, the last minister of culture, because that one hated Americans and helped build the Pompidou Center. Negulesco is eighty-six and is called the father of CinemaScope. He directed *How to Marry a Millionaire*, the first movie to tell a simple story in widescreen without diverting attention from the forty-foot expanse of Marilyn Monroe's knockers. Fellow director Richard Brooks, ten years Negulesco's junior, listens to the ceremony as we flag down waiters carrying trays of champagne glasses meant for guests of the minister. We drink only half of each, then request a colder one. Six half-glasses into the presentation, with no end in sight, Brooks leaps up from the fancy crowd (he wears tennis shoes and a short-sleeved gingham shirt) and says to the minister of culture: "That's an awfully long speech for such a short ribbon."

Pouring rain. Elaine hires a stretch Mercedes and she, Jack the singing playwright, and I are driven to Paris. Elaine speaks French but her driver speaks English. We go to lunch at Brasserie Lipp, and she orders a sausage smothered in mayonnaise so yellow it looks like mustard. I taste it. After lunch we go antiquing. Find a foot-high plaster Charlie Chaplin statue in a shuttered store, and hunt down shopkeeper, who lets me in and says Charlot's mine for $500. He's down to $425 by the time I'm holding the thing, noticing it's marked on the bottom *1930, New York*. It's $400 by the time it goes back to the shelf. Elaine invites me to dinner at L'Orangerie and a transvestite show afterward at the Alcazar, but I've seen and eaten enough and take last flight out to London, where the people speak English, where the movies are new, and where I spend the night vomiting my brains out, convinced it was the sausage, not the mayonnaise. **Q**

CYNTHIA KOLBOWSKI *to* Q

When my mother was eighteen years old, she worked for the first ballpoint pen company in Argentina. It was 1945. Juan Perón was mounting a military coup. Every week she spent her paycheck on clothes: broad-shouldered suits with narrow skirts. She'd copy designs from Hollywood films and take them to her *modista.* She looked like a movie star, though at home she shared a bed with her sister.

Her parents were émigré Russians. My grandfather made hats. My mother was never without a hat. She suffered over hair too thin and permed it too often. Hours spent before the mirror like before the screen, trying to read her future in her face.

My father would sooner dress sharply than eat. It was upward mobility for them, as if they were born to it, as if it ran in their blood straight to their heads. You are what you look like, he'd say. And my father brought his sharp suits to New York City and paced Forty-seventh Street with a gold watch so finely crafted that no one believed he'd made it.

Picture him on the deck of an Atlantic freighter in 1949. He looks at the sky for hours, does nothing, thinks. He's in it for two months, this trip, and it passes too slowly. He thinks about another trip, from Poland to Argentina. He's five years old and the captain's pet. The crew gives him tours of the engineering room. Now he plays cards with the crew; he gets bored, stands on the deck for hours thinking. It tears me up, this image of my father bored.

This is my mother on her honeymoon in Mendoza. She wears dark sunglasses and a riding habit. She looks beautiful, athletic, trim in her outfit. In the background is a Spanish villa. She knows this is a special time. My father knows he must record it. This is my father on the steps of the Opera. He wears a double-breasted suit with wide lapels. He is so thin. His pants are pleated, wide in the leg, cuffed at the ankle. He wears a woolen vest and fashionable dark glasses. He knows nothing of the New York winter to come. Now he has his jeweler's shop on the Avenida Libertador. He makes watches. My mother wears a golden spiral that wraps around her wrist and ends in a sphere with a dome-shaped crystal. And my father wears my mother on his arm. It's 1945. Perón has been elected President. But soon he's in a military prison.

I can see my father alone in New York. He speaks little English; no one is hiring. Sometimes he spends a whole day at the Paramount watching the shows. My mother writes him love letters in ballpoint pen. He takes self-portraits with his camera on a timer and sends them to us.

But why did he go to New York?
You had portraits of Juan and Evita hanging above your crib, says my grandmother. Everyone in Buenos Aires was wearing watches and hats.
And the next day they held out their hats for coins, says my grandfather; he lost the shop.

My mother's father is Russian, but he looks like a gaucho, like a true Latino. He has shiny black hair greased back in the style of the time. He has a thick black mustache, which he grooms with great care. And the wide mouth beneath it is so perfect it's as if he modeled it as well with his scissors and comb. I am four years old, and he takes me to the factory where he works and fashions a hat for me. He tells me my mother went to join my father in the States, but the letters keep coming addressed to her.

My grandfather's undershirts have holes in them but my grandmother refuses to mend them. She is certain that this way he would never remove his shirt in front of another woman. Sophia, *por favor!* he cries. She shrugs, as though helpless against her own stubbornness.

I study my parents' wedding album. It is a silent movie: my mother applying lipstick; my mother lowering her veil. My father stepping out of a car in top hat, talis, and tails. The guests arrive; the wedding party assembles before the rabbi. Everyone is very serious. My parents sip wine and crush the glass in a linen napkin. The first smile is my mother's. She holds a long knife poised above a three-tiered cake and grins at my father. But the camera catches her eyes mid-blink and she appears almost sinister. In the next frame my father guides her hands as she makes the first cut and her face dissolves into laughter.

But why was my mother abducted?
It was the military, says my grandmother.
It was the *Perónistas,* says my grandfather.

My father says nothing, because I don't ask him. I go to see him at the factory where he works. He looks old. He is soldering the casing of a watch and he doesn't look up. He doesn't approve of me, of my life, of my clothes, of my underground activities. I wonder if he can see my mother in me. I think of her posing demurely for his camera. She wears a gown of her own design. It has a black velvet strapless bodice and a broad taffeta skirt. I imagine my father in black tie, holding the camera, framing the picture, and I look at myself, at my clothes, at my thin hair, and I look at my father, who doesn't look up.

This is him playing croquet, a gentleman's game. Bending over his mallet he turns his face to the camera three-quarters and smiles. This is my mother in Mar del Plata. She leans against a column, one leg straight, one bent at the knee. Her hands are behind her back, palms flat against the marble. This is my father in the Plaza de Mayo, where only a few days before thousands of *descamisados,* shirtless ones, demanded and won the release of Perón. I look at a studio portrait of my mother at sixteen, trying to read my future in her face. **Q**

My father always wore the most beautiful clothes when we went riding together. In particular, I remember his hunting coat, which was the color of dried blood and had a pocket inside for dead rabbits.

He took me to the museum to see the pictures of horses. The camera had frozen them in mid-gallop. The pictures were arranged in strips of frames, like movies' film. My father said that before they had invented a fast enough shutter, no one knew that a galloping horse lifts all its hooves from the ground at once. My father pointed to the frame that had proved this point. The horse did not look as if it was galloping with all its hooves in the air. The horse looked perfectly still, all sliced up in time like that.

On my birthday, my father took me to a special place. We had to drive a long way. The stable where I usually rode was a place of hard-mouthed ponies, snoozing dogs, fleas. This place wasn't a riding school, it was an academy. It was immaculately clean; I had never seen horses surrounded by such cleanliness. I suppose it must have been the sort of place where my father rode when he was a child. My father looked perfect leaning against the spotless wood in his jodhpurs and boots, his coat.

My father said, "Ride any horse you want."

The lady who ran the stable showed me a pony she thought I would like. It was like all the other ponies I had ever ridden: barrel-chested, gentlemanly, wise in its way.

I had cantered. I had ridden over the cantilevered bars. It was my ambition that day to gallop.

In the stall next to the pony, a big horse was waving his head around. He was the color of a blue-black bruise.

I said, "I want to ride him."

My father said, "Now that you're ten, I trust you to make

decisions. I think in this case we both know what the wise decision is."

I said, "You promised—any horse." I knew I had him. My father was always as good as his word.

They had to lift me on that horse, he was so tall. My father said he would put a lead line between our horses when we got onto the trail. The lead line would connect our horses' bits so that my horse could not bolt. I felt it was an indignity to be attached to my father by means of this equestrian umbilical cord.

We rode out to the rings. When my father held out his arm to snap the lead line on to my horse's snaffle, I reined my horse's head from my father's hand.

I said, "First I'm going to go into the ring. Alone."

I guess my father was too surprised to say anything. He continued to lean toward me, holding out the lead line.

I rode away from my father and into the ring. The minute I was in the ring, the horse yanked his head so that the reins flew from my fingers. The horse took off in a gallop and I lost my stirrups. The only thing to hold on to was his mane; my hands were my anchors as I bounced high in the air.

The horse went around the ring once, past my father, who was yelling something I could not hear. I was not as much afraid of falling off as of being stuck forever on that horse, going around and around the ring. If that happened, my father would have to bring me a sandwich every day and hold it out at arm's length so I could grab it as I went by. My poor father would have to come every day, that long drive.

The next time the horse went around the ring, he headed straight for the stable, oblivious of the fence which stood in his way. In fact, he galloped even faster, if such a thing was possible. He made that *huh huh huh* sound. His neck was straight out, like a wooden plank. Right before the fence, he planted his feet and tucked his head in. I rolled along his neck and BAM!

Down on the ground, all I could see was hooves and dust. The hooves were hitting the ground like bombs. They raised dust in great puffs. I was in a desert being bombed. I could see my tiny, faraway father jumping off his horse.

The next instant my father was helping me up, the horse grazing beside us. My father reached into the pocket inside his coat, the pocket in which he used to keep dead rabbits. But all my father pulled out was a handkerchief and all he did was wipe my face.

My father said, "I wanted to help you. I couldn't do anything. I just couldn't do anything. I tried to, but I couldn't do anything." He kept saying things like that.

That night my father read me a story about elves. They dance inside mushroom circles called "elf rings." If you wander into one of these, you will be trapped inside and the elves will dance you around until you die.

When I went to bed, I noticed a bruise blooming on my hip. It was in the oval shape of the ring in which I had ridden that day. That bruise seemed a mark, a judgment against me.

As I drifted off, I wondered why my father hadn't simply used the camera from the museum to stop the horse. I thought that tomorrow I would ask him to use the camera to stop me from growing up.

It did not work; he could not help me. It seems to me that I am always in that ring now, going around and around on that horse that nothing can stop, not the shutter of a camera, not my father. I can see my father, my poor little father, obligingly holding out the sandwich, the sandwich he takes from the inside pocket of his coat, the pocket in which he used to keep dead rabbits. **Q**

I only
know
one way
to
act

I want a repeat performance

Łu @ '87